Clutterfree
with
Kids

change your thinking | discover new habits | free your home

JOSHUA BECKER

*For every parent who desires a better life
for themselves and their children.*

Contents

Introduction

Nobody really believes possessions equal joy. In fact, if specifically asked the question, nobody in their right mind would ever say the secret to a joyful life is to own a lot of stuff. Deep down, nobody really thinks it's true. Yet almost all of us live like it is.

From the moment we are born, we are told to pursue more. Advertisements from every television, radio, newspaper, magazine, billboard, and website scream to us on a daily basis that more is better. As a result, we spend countless hours comparing our things to the person next to us. We measure our family's success by the wealth of our belongings. And we end up looking for jobs that pay enough money so we can spend our adult lives purchasing the biggest homes, fanciest cars, trendiest fashions, most popular toys, and coolest technologies.

But we all know it's not true. We all know happiness cannot be bought at a department store. More is not necessarily better. We've just been told the lie so many times we begin to believe it—without even noticing.

Consider some of these statistics:

•The average American cardholder carries 3.7 credit cards.[1]

•The average American household carries over $15,000 in credit card debt.[2]

•The average U.S. household debt is 136 percent of household income, which means the typical American family owes more money than it makes in an entire year.[3]

• The number of shopping centers in the U.S. surpassed the number of high schools back in 1987.[4]

•The average size of the American home has more than doubled over the past 50 years.[5]

•One out of every 10 households in our country rents a storage unit to house their excess belongings.[6]

We live in a world that loves accumulating possessions. And while nobody would ever admit they are trying to purchase happiness, most people live like they are.

But what if there was a better way to live life? One that recognizes the empty promises of advertisements and consumerism. One that champions the pursuit of living with only the most essential possessions needed for life. One that boldly declares there is more joy in owning less than can be found in pursuing more.

That truth would change everything about us. It would change the way we spend our hours, our energy, and our money. It would change where we focus our attention and our minds. It would change the very foundation of our lives.

In short, it would free us to pursue the things in life of lasting value. It would be a completely life-changing and life-giving realization. And it may just line up with everything your heart, deep down, has been telling you all along.

Section 1
Change Your Thinking

[1]
What My 5-Year Old Son Taught Me about Organization

"Simplicity, clarity, singleness: These are the attributes that give our lives power and vividness and joy."
—Richard Holloway

If you had told me years ago I'd be writing a book for parents about living clutterfree, I would have said you were crazy.

And if I didn't have the chance to say it, my wife would have told you for me. We had been together for too many years, she knew me too well, and organizing was not in my blood. It was painfully obvious.

I've lived most of my life as a terribly disorganized person. And to make it worse, I'm a bit of a pack rat by nature and way too forgetful for my own good. Every morning, if I wasn't searching for my car keys, I was looking for my shoes, my belt, or my watch. Chances were, they were never in the place they belonged and even if they were, I would have never thought to check there first.

But five years ago, everything changed. A light-bulb clicked. And I owe it all to a 5-year old.

Now, I write about simplicity and organization full-time on my blog, *Becoming Minimalist*. I've promoted living with less on television, radio, newspaper, and various venues all around the world. I stand as living proof that anybody can become an organized person, live clutterfree, and find a better, more-freeing life because of it.

But for me, it started with an incredibly important lesson I learned one morning while trying to clean out my garage with my son.

I remember it quite well. It was a spring weekend in Vermont. I woke up early that Saturday with one goal in mind: clean the garage. After the long, cold winter, I knew it was going to be an all-day project. So I set my alarm early to get a good start.

My wife and I had decided to spend our spring weekend cleaning the house from top to bottom. After all, that's what disorganized (and organized) families do in the springtime, right? And we were, by definition, just your standard, run-of-the-mill, middle-class family of four living in the suburbs.

The project started harmlessly enough as we set out to begin cleaning the garage. I invited my son to help me not because I thought he'd be super-helpful, but because I wanted to spend some time with him after working all week. For some reason, I thought he'd enjoy pulling out everything from the garage, hosing it down, and moving everything back in. Boy, was I mistaken.

If I recall correctly, he lasted about four minutes (and that may be on the generous side). To be fair, he did pull out one blue bin full of summer toys. But while reaching for the next plastic bin, he noticed his baseball bat and whiffle ball. And he decided to quit. He grabbed his bat and ball, looked me in the eye, and said, "Can I go to the backyard and play?"

Reluctantly, I agreed as I headed back into the garage to grab more stuff. I lamented the fact that the quality time I had hoped to spend with him lasted only four minutes.

Nearly three hours later, I was still working on the same garage—my son still in the backyard, now swinging on the swing set. My neighbor, who happened to be outside working on her home at the same time, noticed my growing frustration. She turned to me and said sarcastically, "Oh, the joys of home ownership."

I responded by saying, "Well, you know what they say, 'The more stuff you own, the more your stuff owns you'." Her next sentence struck a chord with my mind, heart, and soul. It eventually changed the course of my life forever.

She responded, "Yeah, that's why my daughter is a *minimalist*. She keeps telling me I don't need all this stuff!"

I had never heard the word *minimalist* before. But after working all morning in my garage, it sounded surprisingly attractive. And in that moment, everything changed.

My son...my garage...my growing frustration...it all started to make sense and pointed to one incredibly valuable, life-changing lesson: *Living life is more enjoyable than managing and organizing stuff!*

It was the lesson my 5-year old son knew far better than me and had tried to teach me when he ran into the backyard.

But I didn't see it. At least, not until my neighbor identified the roadblocks keeping me from that type of freedom.

Life would be better lived if there was less stuff to manage and organize and clean. Not only were my possessions not bringing me joy. They were actually distracting me from the very things that did. And a minimalist was born.

Along with my wife and two kids, we immediately began going through each room, closet, and drawer in our home; removing as many unneeded items as possible. The goal was to live with only the possessions we needed or loved. And from that day forward, rather than seeking to live with more and more stuff in our home, we have tried to live with less and less.

As a result, we have found cleaning to be easier, organizing to be less painful, and managing our life less stressful. We have discovered more time to be together and more opportunity to live life in the backyard, rather than cleaning out the garage.

Suddenly, living clutterfree didn't seem so difficult. Drawers had plenty of room. Closets had space to breathe. Toy rooms were less crowded. Clean-up was a snap. And the house almost always looked cleaned.

I became an organized person with a passion to inspire others to live more life by owning less stuff. And my 5-year old son had held the secret all along. Living life is indeed far more enjoyable than managing and organizing stuff!

You will find numerous themes throughout the pages of this book designed to inspire and equip you as a parent to live clutterfree. But many of them rest on a simple, important premise: *There is more joy to be found in owning less than can ever be found in organizing more.*

This is a foundational understanding that is rare in our culture. Our society has trained us to think just the opposite. For that reason, it is important to take a step back and rethink our passion for possessions.

[2]
How Simplicity Leads to Better Living

"Happiness resides not in possessions, and not in gold,
happiness dwells in the soul." —Democritus

Don't Just Declutter, De-Own.

It is better to own less than to organize more.

As we live our lives, especially with kids in the house, we consistently find more and more things entering our home. Holidays, birthdays, schoolwork, shopping, and passing fads contribute to this reality. On an almost daily basis, things enter into our home.

Unfortunately, rarely do we create opportunities to discard of them. As a result, our homes fill with more and more stuff. And because we believe the best solution is to find organizational tools to manage all of it, we seek out bigger containers or more efficient organizational tips and tricks.

But simply organizing our stuff (without removing it) is always only a temporary solution. By definition, organizing possessions is an action that must be repeated over and over and over again. It is simply rearranging. And though we may find storage solutions today, we are quickly forced to find new ones as early as tomorrow.

Additionally, merely organizing our stuff has major shortcomings that are rarely considered.

Organization does not benefit anyone else. The possessions we rarely use sit on shelves in our basements, attics, and garages—even while some of our closest friends desperately need them.

Organization does not turn back our desire for more. The simple act of organizing our things into boxes, plastic bins, or extra closets does not turn back our desire to purchase more things. The culture-driven inclination to find happiness in our possessions is rarely thwarted in any meaningful way through the process of simple organization.

Organization does not force us to evaluate our lives. While rearranging our stuff may cause us to look at each of our possessions, it does not force us to evaluate them—especially if we are just putting them in boxes and closing the lids. On the other hand, intentionally removing possessions from our home forces questions of passion, values, and what's most important to us.

Organization does not solve our financial problems. Organization, in and of itself, never addresses the underlying issue that we buy too much stuff. In fact, many times, the act of rearranging our stuff costs us even more as we purchase containers, storage units, or larger homes to house it.

Organization accomplishes little in paving the way for other changes. Organizing may provide a temporary lift to our attitude. It clears a room and subsequently clears our mind, but it rarely paves the way for healthy, major lifestyle changes. Our house is too small, our income is too little, and we still can't find enough time in the day. We may have rearranged our stuff, but not our lives.

On the other hand, the act of removing possessions from our home accomplishes many of the purposes above. It is not a temporary solution that must be repeated. It is an act of permanence. Once an item has been removed, it is removed completely.

Whether we re-sell our possessions, donate them to charity, or give them to a friend, they are immediately put to use by those who need them. Removing possessions begins to turn back our desire for more as we find freedom, happiness, and abundance in owning less. And removing ourselves from the all-consuming desire to own more creates opportunity for significant life changes to take place.

As you seek to free your home and create a clutterfree environment over the course of this book, challenge yourself often to remove the unneeded things in your home. Rid yourself of the extra weight in a permanent manner. As you move from room to room, carry a donation box, a recycle bin, or create a garage sale pile. It does not matter so much how you remove them, as long as you do.

It is far better to de-own than declutter—which is one reason I have fallen in love with the message of minimalism.

Introduction to Minimalism and Owning Less.

For the past several years, I have written a blog called *Becoming Minimalist*. It is a website written to inspire others to live more by owning less. It is not based on a rigid approach to minimalism, but encourages each reader to discover a rational style of minimalism unique to their lifestyle.

Often times, I am asked the seemingly simple question, "So what is minimalism anyway?"

It is a question received from many different angles — sometimes from people I have just met, other times from people I have known for many years. Either way, I typically answer with a short explanation, "It is a lifestyle where people intentionally seek to live with only the things they really need."

It is a simple answer that briefly sums up the lifestyle. But secretly, I always desire to answer more in-depth. I know minimalism runs far deeper than merely living with fewer possessions. And I always hope they will ask follow-up questions that allow me to explain the lifestyle further.

Minimalism is about intentionality. It is marked by clarity, purpose, and thoughtfulness. At its core, *minimalism is the intentional promotion of the things we most value and the removal of everything that distracts us from it.* It is a life that forces intentionality upon us. And as a result, it forces improvements in almost all aspects of our lives.

Minimalism is freedom from the passion to possess. Modern society has bought into the lie that the good life is found in accumulating things—in possessing as much as possible. They believe more is always better and have inadvertently subscribed to the idea that happiness can be purchased at a department store. But they are wrong. Minimalism brings freedom from the all-consuming passion to possess. It steps off the treadmill of consumerism and dares to seek happiness elsewhere. It values relationships, experiences, and soul-care. And in doing so, it finds life.

Minimalism is freedom from the modern rush. Our world lives at a feverish pace. We are too hurried, too frenzied, and too stressed. We work long, passionate hours to pay the bills, but fall deeper into debt. We rush from one activity to another—multitasking along the way—but never seem to get everything done. We remain in constant connection with others through our cell phones, but true life-changing relationships continue to elude us. Minimalism slows down life and frees us from this modern hysteria to live faster. It finds freedom to disengage. It seeks to remove the frivolous and keep the significant. And in doing so, it values the intentional endeavors that add value to life.

Minimalism is countercultural. We live in a world that idolizes celebrities. They are photographed for magazines, interviewed on the radio, and recorded for television. Their lives are held up as the golden standard and are envied by many. People who live minimalist lives are not championed by the media in the same way. They don't fit into the consumerist culture promoted by corporations and politicians. Yet, they live a life that is attractive and inviting. While most people are chasing after success, glamour, and fame, minimalism calls out to us with a smaller, quieter, calmer voice. It invites us to slow down, consume less, but enjoy more. And when we meet someone living a simplified life, we often recognize we have been chasing the wrong things all along.

Minimalism is both external and internal. In my first book, *Simplify*, I outline 7 guiding principles to help anyone declutter their home and life. The principles in the book have helped tens of thousands find freedom by removing much of the physical clutter in their home. The book concentrates almost exclusively on the externals of life. Designed to help people find freedom from external clutter, just like this one, it opens the door for people to also find freedom in their heart and soul. After the external clutter has been removed, minimalism creates space to address the deepest heart issues that impact our relationships and life.

Minimalism is completely achievable. Too many will quit before they even start. But a minimalist life is achievable. My family stands as living proof. We were the typical definition of a family of four living in the suburbs accumulating as much stuff as our income and credit cards would allow. But we have since embraced an intentional lifestyle of living with less. No magic potion needed. And we will never return to our old way of life. We stand as living proof that minimalism is completely achievable (and unique) to anyone who seeks it.

Those who are genuinely interested in knowing what minimalism is and what it represents are drawn to the principles of the lifestyle. After all, it offers almost everything our heart has been asking for all along.

The benefits of living with less are relevant, practical, and life-giving. And they are worthy of exploration.

Benefits of Owning Less.

We own too much stuff. And it is stealing our joy.

Consider how our possessions deplete our most finite and valuable resources:

Money. Everything we buy moves our financial balance closer to zero—sometimes even below. The Average American with credit card debt lives with $15,956 debt spread out over 3.5 credit cards.[7] But it is not only families with debt that struggle. Recent statistics report nearly 8 out of every 10 Americans live paycheck-to-paycheck.[8]

Time. Our possessions rob us of precious minutes every day. They are required to be cleaned, organized, maintained, fixed, recycled, removed, and replaced. And that doesn't even begin to account for all the time we spent working in the first place just to earn the money to buy the possessions that we take home to be cleaned and organized and maintained and...

Energy. Our excessive possessions demand our attention and mental energy. Clutter in our life contends for our eyes, our attention, and our focus. Our minds are subtly consumed with the pursuit of possessions—and the temptation to compare our possessions with those around us permeates our thoughts more than we'd like to admit.

But there is a far better way to live life. The removal of excessive possessions and the intentional decision to live with less offers countless benefits. In exchange for removing the clutter, we are rewarded with newfound finances, time, energy, freedom, and mental capacity. Our lives are lived with less stress, less anxiety, and less burden.

Life is immediately improved. Our finite resources become more available to us. We are freed to pursue our greatest passions. And for some of us, it's been a long time since we had access to the necessary finite resources required to chase our heart's greatest delights—however we decide to define them.

For too long, we've bought into the lie that more is better. We've bought trendier clothes and cooler toys—clutter has accumulated. But we've traded far more than time and money to acquire them. We've traded the very passions and life we most desperately desire to pursue.

But they can be rediscovered.

Living with less provides more time to spend on meaningful activities and more freedom to travel and move about.

Living with less provides more clarity in our spiritual pursuits and more mental capacity to solve problems in life.

Living with less provides more finances to support causes we believe in. And it provides greater flexibility to pursue the careers we most desire.

Owning fewer possessions provides the perfect roadmap for living the life we've always dreamed of living. Maybe for the first time. Finally.

The Heart Impact of Less.

Our decision to own less occurred in a moment standing in my driveway. But digging deeper into the story would reveal and expose several streams of discontent evidenced in my life for a number of years.

I had lived most of my married life discontent with the use of our finances. While never deep in debt, I was tired of living paycheck-to-paycheck despite numerous income increases over the years. I always had a strong internal desire to help others with my finances, but was handcuffed by my spending.

Another stream of discontent included the focus of my life's energy. I was becoming increasingly frustrated that I couldn't find more time and energy to be with my family and the people that mattered most. Somehow, I had been unable to notice my desire to own possessions was the cause of this discontent in my life. Luckily, my neighbor pointed it out in dramatic fashion.

My life forever changed. Owning less provided opportunity to redirect time, energy, and money towards the things that matter most. Ultimately, it brought great resolution to the discontent listed above.

It provided an even greater opportunity to change than I had ever imagined. The outward change of behavior brought along with it the opportunity for inward change as well. It has allowed my heart to adopt the very values I always admired in others.

For example, consider how the intentional decision to live with fewer possessions allows our hearts to embrace some very desirable qualities.

Contentment: *being mentally or emotionally satisfied with things as they are.* So much of the discontent in our lives revolves around physical possessions and comparing our things to others. An intentional decision to live with less allows this discontent to slowly fade.

Generosity: *willingness and liberality in giving away one's money, time, etc.* When the selfish, hoarder-based mentality is removed from our thinking, we are free to use our resources for other purposes. We are allowed (and have more opportunity) to redirect our energy, time, and money elsewhere.

Gratitude: *a feeling of thankfulness or appreciation.* One of the most important steps we can take towards experiencing gratitude is to think less about the things we don't possess and more about the things we do. Intentionally living with less provides that opportunity.

Self-Control: *the ability to exercise restraint or control over one's feelings, emotions, reactions, etc.* Many people go through life having no clear sense of their true values. Instead, their desires are molded by the culture and the advertisements that bombard them each day. As a result, they find no consistency in life. No self-control. The decision to live our own lives apart from an ever-shifting culture provides opportunity for self-control to emerge.

Honesty: *honorable in principles, intentions, and actions; upright and fair.* Many—not all, but many—of the lies and mistruths in our world are based in a desire to get ahead and possess more. Finding contentment with our life eliminates the need to be dishonest for financial or social gain.

Appreciation: *the act of estimating the qualities of things and giving them their proper value.* As the desires of our life stop focusing on others and what they have that we don't, we are more able to appreciate their accomplishment, their success, and the beauty they bring to the world. We are able to fully appreciate others without being jealous of them (or worse, hoping for their downfall).

Now, please don't misread me. I am not contending that those who choose to live with less automatically become more content, generous, grateful, or honest than others. I know many incredibly generous people who would not describe themselves as minimalist. I'm sure there are some self-defined minimalists who would chart obnoxiously high on the selfishness meter. And I would never self-confess to have arrived fully in any of the categories listed above.

But I have come to realize the intentional rejection of possessions does allow greater opportunity for these positive heart habits to emerge. What you do with that opportunity is up to you.

Rethinking the Obstacles to Minimalism.

Minimalists come in all sizes, ages, genders, races, nationalities, social classes, and religions. It is a growing movement that continues to invite others to live with less and define their lives in greater ways than by the things they own. Yet, despite its recent growth, it continues to be misunderstood in a number of important ways.

In fact, if you picked up this book with the hopes of just discovering some quick and easy tips to live clutterfree with kids, you may be asking yourself why there is so much emphasis at the beginning about living with less. If this is the first you've heard about minimalism, you may be experiencing some hesitation. Likely, these hesitations are based on one or more common misconceptions.

With that in mind, it is important to address some of these common misconceptions about minimalism.

Owning less is stark and barren. One of our first projects after becoming minimalist was to go through the house and remove every decoration that was not meaningful or beautiful. But we didn't remove every decoration in the house, only the ones that didn't mean anything to us. By the end, every decoration in our home held significance to our lives. And because of that, our guests can immediately recognize what is most important to us. Our walls are not barren. They are filled with life—our lives.

Owning less will be boring. A minimalist life is not void of excitement or entertainment. In fact, minimalism removes many of the mundane tasks (organizing, shopping, cleaning) that rob us of daily excitement. When unnecessary possessions have been removed, we are freed to choose for ourselves what types of things will define our lives. Some will choose to travel the world, spice up their family life, find a new career, or just spend more time at home.

Owning less means I can't own nice things. One of the greatest unforeseen benefits of living a minimalist life is the opportunity to purchase possessions of higher quality. For some reason, many people don't correlate owning fewer things and owning nicer things. But the truth is, they go hand-in-hand and are directly related. When a commitment is made to buy fewer things, our lives are opened to the opportunity of owning nicer things as well.

Owning less is only for lazy people. I'll be the first to admit that some people use minimalism as a means to live a lazy, selfish, unproductive life. But that does not define the majority of minimalists I know. Most minimalists carry the same responsibilities (work, family, society) as those who are not minimalist. And while some have certainly embraced minimalism as a means to quit their day job, most do it simply as a means to pursue passions they love. And I think that's a great thing.

Owning less is just for extreme environmentalists. Minimalism is good for the environment. Minimalists consume less resources and discard less resources. And that benefits everybody. But not everyone who embraces minimalism does so out of environmental motivations. Personally speaking, my embrace of minimalism was rooted in discontent with the path of my life. In minimalism, I found more opportunity to live out my greatest values and just because those decisions contribute to the health of the planet along the way doesn't mean it was a driving force in the decision.

Owning less means I must sacrifice sentimentality. We will spend an entire chapter on the organization of sentimental possessions a bit later. For now, understand that less is different than none. Personally, my family finds more value in sentimental belongings if we pull out the most important pieces and keep them in a significant place. As a result, rather than a box full of sentimental things stuck in the basement, we display the most important pieces from our past somewhere in our home. In that way, owning less actually promotes the memories most valuable to us.

Owning less means I can never entertain. Making a positive difference in our community and the lives of others has always been important to my family and will continue to be so as long as we live. Hospitality is something both my wife and I cherish and feel obliged to offer. To accomplish that, we host groups of people in our home almost every week. Owning less does not mean we can no longer entertain. In fact, in some ways, it actually makes it easier (for example: getting the house ready for guests).

Owning less is mean to kids. Kids need toys. They play an important role in establishing intelligence, maturity, teamwork, and worldview. I have not met a single minimalist who denies their child the privilege of owning toys. I have met many who limit the number of toys their children own because teaching the value of boundaries allows them to flourish. And that is the very opposite of cruelty. More on toys a little bit later as well

Minimalism is the intentional promotion of the things we most value and the removal of everything that distracts from it. It is a highly personal journey that forces us to identify and articulate our highest values. Because of that, it is always going to be practiced differently by each individual.

No wonder minimalists come in all ages, genders, races, nationalities, social classes, and religions. No wonder it is a growing movement that helps others define their lives in greater ways than the things they own.

And no wonder it is the most important step to living clutterfree you will ever take.

[3]
Parenting Over Possessions

"I cannot believe that the purpose of life is to be happy. I think the purpose of life is to be useful, to be responsible, to be compassionate. It is, above all to matter, to count, to stand for something, to have made some difference that you lived at all." —Leo Rosten

We Are All Trading Our Lives. Trade Up.

Our lives are, by definition, made up of finite resources. Each of us has a limited amount of minutes, dollars, and units of energy with which to live our lives. Every passing day presents an opportunity to trade our lives for something else. This is one of the reasons creating a clutterfree environment is so important—it creates the space necessary to live intentionally.

Unfortunately, most of our lives are unintentionally traded down and lived in exchange for a return of limited or temporal value. We never set out to purposefully trade our lives for things of limited value; but in a culture surrounded by similar pursuits, our lives conform too easily.

At the very beginning, we trade our lives for...

Security. We invest in our knowledge and skill as a means to earn a living. We choose the lives we will live. We seek the right people to place around us. And we trade our time and talents for a steady paycheck with which to purchase shelter, clothing, food—security, the baseline of our existence. Make no mistake, this is not an unwise trade.

Security lays the foundation upon which many of our life's choices can be built. And I'm all for it. But it seems, after achieving security, most of us begin pursuing...

Comfort. The essential elements of security: roof, meals, clothing are rarely enough. We pursue comfort to be added to our baseline of security. So we begin trading our time and our paychecks for a bigger home in a nicer neighborhood, a softer couch surrounded by entertainment choices, a nicer car with more features, and trendier clothing that makes us feel a bit more fashionable among our peers. Sometimes we intentionally seek comfort; but most often we do so because society makes it appear so attractive.

Luxury. After achieving security and comfort, luxury lurks not so far in the distance. We can see it. We can taste it. It appears overwhelmingly satisfying, and, we know what it asks of us: just a few more hours each week at work, a little more research to get it right, and a few more dollars spent at the store. Soon, we begin trading the finite resources of our lives for the luxurious offerings of this world.

Victory. Our minds create a ranking system for the world that we desire to climb. We seek more money, more power, more prestige, more fame than our neighbor, our siblings, our friends, or those we read about in the news. We attempt to prove our worth to ourselves and others by beating out others in this self-constructed competition of life. And before we know it, we've soon traded our entire lives to win a competition we have invented in our own minds.

Of course, none of these pursuits exist in a vacuum. Each of them thrive in our hearts alongside a steady stream of pride, greed, fear, and selfishness. These emotions reinforce our decision to pursue comfort, luxury, and victory. As a result, we seek them more desperately. And our lives' most valuable resources are traded for them.

But the trade is a foolish one.

Our lives hold far greater potential than the comfort and luxury most of us trade for them. After all, these are temporal pursuits that can never be fully achieved. They move and shift rapidly with the world around us. They never fully satisfy. They are completely self-centered. And our lives can be traded for things far greater.

Our lives can be traded for significance, social justice, or spiritual pursuits. We can invest our lives into creating a more sustainable planet, beautiful art, moments of joy for others, causes we believe in, or raising responsible children. We can help others overcome fear, heartache, or significant obstacles to joy. We can trade our finite resources for the desires and values held deep within our hearts—the purest passions unspoiled by the culture around us.

We were created to live for pursuits greater than comfort, luxury, and competition. We were created to trade our lives up, not down.

The Example We Set.

An interesting story is told of Monterey, California, a coastal town, that quickly became a pelican's paradise. As the local fishermen returned each day to clean their fish, they would fling the unused internal organs of the fish to the pelicans. The birds graciously accepted their gift and as a result, quickly grew fat, lazy, and contented. Eventually however, when the fishing industry in Monterey took a downturn, the free meals began to slow for the pelicans.

When the change came, the pelicans made no effort to fish for themselves. Instead, they waited around and grew gaunt and thin. Many even starved to death. Because of the free handouts, they had forgotten how to fish for themselves.

To remedy the situation, an unprecedented solution was sought: import new pelicans from the south accustomed to foraging for themselves. These new birds were placed among their starving cousins, and the newcomers immediately started catching fish. Before long, the hungry pelicans followed suit, and the famine was ended.

My son is now 11 and my daughter is 7. Right now, and for a little while longer, we live together as a family. This, then, represents my great opportunity to prepare them for life. Whether we like it or not, our children are soaking up values from us as parents about how to live, how to work, and how to achieve significance. We serve as their most trusted examples for life.

Embracing a life content with fewer possessions has modeled for them the important truths that personal belongings are not the key to happiness, that security is found in their character, and that the pursuit of happiness runs a different road than the pursuit of possessions. These are, of course, valuable life lessons they will never learn in a world that often promises short-term happiness in ready-wrapped packages.

There are countless truths I desire to pass on to my children: being content with less is among the most important.

Since embracing the principles of minimalism, I am overjoyed at some of the lessons my children have learned. They have learned:

They don't need to buy things to be happy. We own far fewer things than we did years ago. We purchase far fewer things than we did years ago. Yet, we are far happier than we were years ago. Go figure.

They don't need to live life like everyone else. Even though they are not quite old enough to understand all of the intricacies of our minimalist life, they completely understand we have made a decision to live differently than most people in our neighborhood. Our lifestyle has given them permission to live a countercultural life.

They can live within their means. Although our children are not balancing our checkbook, they do hear us speak often about debt, the joy of not being in it, and our desire to stay out of it.

They ought to think carefully about their purchases. Because we believe in giving our kids opportunity to find/

grow in their interests, we still need to buy things: toys, school supplies, art supplies, and sporting goods. We just think through our buying decisions more carefully. This is an invaluable lesson for children to learn as they get older. We no longer buy something just because we have the money, we buy things because we need them.

They should gladly share with others. Since we became minimalist when they were young, they have grown up watching us donate many of our belongings to others. They have seen generosity in action.

Clutter is a distraction. They have seen how minimalism creates a home where clutter is scarce. And when it does show up, it can be quickly remedied—and usually is.

The joy of spending time together. Our minimalist home has allowed us the opportunity to spend less time purchasing, cleaning, organizing, and sorting things. We have gladly replaced the time managing stuff with spending time with them.

We are in control of our stuff. Not the other way around.

Providing Lasting Security.

It is human nature to need and desire security. And this sense of security can come either from material goods or from supportive relationships. As a result, researchers point out that people who do not feel loved and accepted by others tend to put a stronger emphasis on material possessions.

Margaret Clark, a professor of psychology at Yale, writes it this way, "Humans are social creatures with vulnerabilities. Close relationships afford protections. For example, infants wouldn't survive without other people. But material possessions also afford protection and security. Humans need food, clothing and shelter to survive. So, it takes a mix of things to make you feel secure. But if you heighten one source of security, people feel less concerned about the others."

This finding was based on two unique research projects she and her colleagues conducted and published in the March 2011 issue of *The Journal of Experimental Social Psychology*. In conclusion, the researchers point out that those who do not feel internally secure in their personal relationships will often put a higher value on physical possessions.

This is an important reality for us as parents to realize and understand. Often times, in our busy, hectic, run-run-run world, we are left with too little time to spend with our children—or the time we do spend with them is at the very end of the day when all of our resources have been used up.

Often, we spend our time and energy chasing things that are physical in nature. We dream of a future that includes larger paychecks and bigger houses. We plot and plan to acquire them. We go to great lengths to care for them and we become jealous when others have more of them. All the while, we convince ourselves we are seeking these things to improve the security and opportunity for our children.

But all of the security found in possessions is fragile and fleeting at best.

The research, and probably our own hearts, argue against this thinking. They call us to remember the importance of things that can not be seen with the naked eye: love, friendship, hope, integrity, trust, compassion. These bring substance, fulfillment, and lasting joy to our lives. And these are the attributes that ultimately bring lasting security to our children's lives.

May we seek and pursue them. And may we provide a foundation of love, acceptance, and quality time with our kids because of it.

Giving Greater Gifts.

I have countless holiday memories. Most of them center on faith, family, and traditions. I remember being excited to see my cousins come in town from Minnesota. I remember my grandparents' living room where the entire family would gather to open presents following a candlelit Christmas Eve service at First Baptist Church in Aberdeen, SD. And I fondly remember playing cards around the kitchen table with my aunts and uncles.

Interestingly enough, looking back, very few holiday memories include the gifts I received. I distinctly remember the year I got a blue dirt bike, the evening my brother and I received a Nintendo, and opening socks every year from my grandparents. Other than that, my gift-receiving memories are pretty sparse. Which got me thinking: What type of gifts can we give to our children they will never forget? What gifts will truly impact their lives and change them forever?

I think I can name a few. Consider this list of gifts we can bestow upon our children that they will never forget:

Affirmation. Sometimes one simple word of affirmation can change an entire life. Make sure your children know how much you appreciate them. Then, remind them every chance you get.

Challenge. Encourage your child to dream big dreams. In turn, they will accomplish more than they thought possible —and probably even more than you thought possible.

Compassion/Justice. Life isn't fair. It never will be—there are just too many variables. But when a wrong has been committed or a playing field can be leveled, I want my child to be active in helping to level it.

Contentment. The need for more is contagious. In a world bent on satisfying every impulse, one of the greatest gifts you can give your children is an appreciation for being content with what they have—while striving to become the best they can be.

Curiosity. Teach your children to ask questions about who, what, where, how, why, and why not. "Stop asking so many questions" are words that should never leave a parents' mouth.

Determination. One of the greatest determining factors in one's success is the size of their will. How can you help grow your child's today?

Discipline. Children need to learn everything from the ground up including appropriate behaviors, how to get along with others, how to get results, and how to achieve their dreams. Discipline should not be avoided or withheld. Instead, it should be consistent and positive.

Faithfulness. Faithfulness in marriage includes more than just our bodies. It also includes our eyes, mind, heart, and soul. Guard your sexuality daily and devote it entirely to your spouse. Your children will absolutely take notice.

Generosity. Teach your children to be generous with your stuff so that they will become generous with theirs.

Honesty/Integrity. Children who learn the value and importance of honesty at a young age have a far greater opportunity to become honest adults. And honest adults who deal truthfully with others tend to feel better about themselves, enjoy their lives more, and sleep better at night.

Hope. Hope is knowing and believing things will get improve. It creates strength, endurance, and resolve. In the desperately difficult times of life, it calls us to press onward.

Imagination. If we've learned anything over the past 20 years, it's that life is changing faster and faster with every passing day. The world tomorrow looks nothing like the world today. The people with imagination are the ones not just living it, they are creating it.

Intentionality. I believe strongly in intentional living and intentional parenting. Slow down, consider who you are, where you are going, and how to get there. Do the same for each of your children.

Lifelong Learning. A passion for learning is different from just studying to earn a grade or please teachers. It begins in the home. So read, ask questions, analyze, and expose. In other words, learn to love learning yourself.

Love. Love is patient. Love is kind. And love endures forever.

Nature. Children who learn to appreciate the world around them take care of the world around them. As a parent, I am frequently asking my kids to keep their rooms inside the house neat, clean, and orderly. Shouldn't we also be teaching them to keep their world outside neat, clean, and orderly?

Opportunity. Kids need opportunities to experience new things so they can find out what they enjoy and what they are good at. Contrary to popular belief, this doesn't have to require much money.

Optimism. Pessimists don't change the world. Optimists do.

Peace. On a worldwide scale, you may think this is out of our hands. But in relation to the people around you, this is completely within your hands—and that's a darn good place to start.

Pride. Celebrate the little things in life. It is the little accomplishments in life that pile up to become the big accomplishments.

Self-Esteem. People who learn to value themselves are more likely to have self-confidence, self-esteem, and self-worth. As a result, they are more likely to become adults who respect their values and stick to them—even when no one else does.

Sense of Humor. Laugh with your children everyday—for their sake and yours.

Spirituality. Faith elevates our view of the universe, our world, and our lives. We would be wise to instill into our kids that they are more than just flesh and blood taking up space. They are also made of mind, heart, soul, and will. And decisions in their life should be based on more than just what everyone else with flesh and blood is doing.

Stability. A stable home becomes the foundation on which children build the rest of their lives. They need to know their place in the family, who they can trust, and who is going to be there for them. Don't keep changing those things.

Time/Undivided Attention. The gift of time is the one gift you can never get back or take back. So think carefully about who (or what) is getting yours.

Uniqueness. What makes us different is what makes us special. Uniqueness should not be hidden. It should be proudly displayed for all the world to see, appreciate, and enjoy.

Of course, none of these gifts are on sale at your local department store. But that's the point. And none of them add clutter to your home either—only warmth.

As parents, investing into our children is one of the most significant pursuits we will ever embrace. It holds benefit for us and our family. The benefit of pursuing significance in this way far outweighs any level of financial success.

Significance over Success.

Financial success is a powerful motivator. It controls the lives of many. It chooses occupations. It dictates how resources are spent. It influences relationships, schedules, and families. To some, it even becomes an all-consuming passion that leaves broken people and morality in its wake.

Unfortunately, it is not the greatest call we have on our lives. In fact, compared to significance, it fades quickly.

There are numerous limitations on financial success.

Success ebbs and flows with the economy. As recent years have proven, financial success is always at the mercy of a national economy and increasingly, a world economy. When the economy takes a downturn (as it always does), so does net worth.

Success ends on the day you die. On the day you die, all wealth and possessions will be immediately transferred to someone else. Even if you get to pick where they go, the reality is that person is always someone other than you.

Success is never enough. Financial success will never satisfy the inmost desires of our soul. No matter the amount of financial success earned, it always leaves us wanting more.

On the other hand, there are other long-lasting pursuits available for us. For example, compare the limitations of financial success to the advantages of significance.

Significance always lasts. Significance will always outlast you. When you are no longer present, your significance will remain. And nothing can ever take that away from you.

Significance carries on. Significance keeps on giving. You positively change the life of another human being…that person changes the life of another…who impacts the life of another…who influences another…

Significance satisfies our soul. While the thirst for success is never quenched, significance satisfies our deepest heart and soul. It allows us to lay our head on our pillow each night confident we lived a valuable and fulfilling day.

Unfortunately, many people spend most of their days and moments chasing financial success. And while some achieve it more than others, almost all find it unfulfilling in the end. When they begin to shift their life focus to significance instead of success, they wonder why they wasted most of their life chasing something different.

Don't waste any of your life. Your children are counting on you. Instead, seek significance starting today.

Realize life won't last forever. Everyone knows life will come to an end—but no one likes to think about it. That's unfortunate. As soon as you start thinking about the end of your life, you begin to live differently in the present. You are never too young to start thinking about your legacy. How do you want people to remember you? And what do you really want to accomplish before you die?

Focus on people, not dollars. Begin to transfer your life's focus from your banking account to the people around you. Rather than worrying about the next get-rich-quick scheme, spend that energy focusing on your child, your neighbor, or the disadvantaged in your community.

Strive to live a life worth copying. Live with character, integrity, and morality. Your life should look the same in private as it does in public. While no one is perfect, begin striving for a life of integrity. It will be noticed by your kids and will shape them for years to come.

Realize that significance is not dependent upon success. Too many people fall into the trap of thinking, "Once I make it rich, I'll become significant." This is rarely the case. Begin striving for it now. If financial success comes your way in the future, your mind will be in a better place to truly use your new success for broader significance.

Reduce your expenses by choosing a more minimalist life. Learn to live with less. Living with less frees up your life to invest into others. And living with reduced expenses allows you the freedom to spend less time at the office and more resources on others.

Find a career outside your job. Sometimes, our day job leads to significance. But if yours does not, find a "career of significance" outside of your employment by volunteering in a local food bank, charity, or nonprofit organization. Most likely, your gifts, talents, or expertise are desperately needed. Use your job to pay the bills, but use your "new career" to pay your soul.

Rarely do people look back on their lives and savor their professional achievements. Instead, they celebrate the impact they have had in the lives of others. Give yourself much to look back on and celebrate. Stop chasing success. Start seeking significance instead.

[4]
The Road to Clutterfree

"Faith is taking the first step even when you don't see the whole staircase." –Martin Luther King, Jr.

Living with Less. You Already Do.

"I will never be able to live clutterfree because I could never intentionally live with less stuff." I've heard it a thousand times.

When I do, I first ask myself, "I wonder what misconception would bring someone to think that? It is always possible." And second, I think to myself, "But you already are living with less. You just don't know it."

The truth of life is this: All of us are already choosing to live with less.

Our resources are finite and limited. Simply put, we can't have it all and we can't do it all. David Allen said it best, *"You can do anything. But you can't do everything."*

Everyday, we trade our lives for something.

When we choose to own fewer possessions, we find more time for the things we love, more money for things of true value, more energy for pursuits of lasting worth, more focus for things that bring real meaning, and more opportunity to pursue our greatest potential.

Intentionally or unintentionally, we are all minimizing something. Many people are choosing to live with less stuff because they realize physical possessions are not adding value to their lives. As a result, they open the doorway for far greater pursuits.

I hope you will consider doing the same.

Inspiration over Instruction.

As I mentioned earlier, I remember in vivid detail the moment we decided to begin living a rational minimalist lifestyle.

At the time, the lifestyle of minimalism was completely foreign to us. It was entirely new in every way. It was unique. The idea of intentionally living with fewer possessions had never been introduced to me. Yet, it sounded surprisingly attractive. It resonated with something deep inside me. And it was quickly embraced by both myself and my wife.

Minimalism offered more than escape from the clutter in our home and lives. It offered the very things our hearts most desperately desired. We jumped in with both feet—and found the water was both warm and refreshing.

Over the next several months and years, we sought to discover what minimalism exactly meant for our family. We knew minimalism was always going to look different for us than it would for others. While not extraordinary, our lives are entirely unique to us.

We lived in the suburbs, so we were going to keep personal transportation. We lived in Vermont, so we were going to keep shovels for the snow and rakes for the autumn leaves. We had kids, so we were going to keep toys and books and games around the house. We enjoyed company, so we would keep enough place settings to comfortably show hospitality.

Minimalism became a journey of experimentation, exploration, and trial-and-error. We were forced to identify our values and articulate what was most important to us.

Since then, I have had the opportunity to speak on minimalism and simplicity in a number of different venues. Each time, I have been asked to give practical help on how to live with less and specific instruction on how to live a more simple life. But each time, I rarely do (or at least, not until the very end).

I was familiar with our journey and the uniqueness of it. And I have found—in my life and in others—the lifestyle of minimalism requires far more inspiration than instruction.

Minimalism is always going to look different from person to person and family to family. Our passions are different. Our personalities are different. Our pasts are different. Our presents are different. As a result, the essentials of our lives are going to change. The principles remain the same, but the specific instructions for decluttering are always going to look a little bit different.

But regardless of the exact differences, we have all been told the exact same mistruths by society. We have all been tricked into thinking the more we own the happier we will be, the more joy we will experience, and the more fulfilled we will be. We've all been fed the same lies countless times since the day we were born. And only the truth about the joy of living with less can counteract that faulty premise.

As a result, the invitation to minimalism is always going to require more inspiration than instruction.

Go Ahead. Get Started With Your Easiest Step.

Typically, when people are introduced to the idea of intentionally owning less, questions begin to arise. Some may question the merit of the lifestyle, but I find that group to be rather small. Most people quickly acknowledge and agree that we own too much stuff.

The questions that arise tend to focus on the specifics— and some very specific specifics at that. Depending on who I am talking to, I may hear one of these questions: "What about my sentimental items and family heirlooms? What about my books? What about my kids' toys? My husband/ wife will never go along with this idea, what should I do with their clutter?"

Interestingly enough, each of these questions sound unique. And in some ways they are, they do represent different personalities and/or family dynamics. But there is one great similarity in each of these questions. And it is this similarity that causes too many people to get stuck in their journey towards a clutterfree home.

Notice, each of these questions represent the apparent "toughest" thing in their homes to declutter: books, heirlooms, or clutter from someone else in the family. Though only introduced to the idea of minimalism, each of their minds has quickly raced to the most difficult area in their home to declutter. And the thought of removing those items from their home seems daunting.

My response to their question is always the same: Take heart, you don't need to start with the hard stuff. Instead, start at the easiest place possible in your home. Build up little victories and momentum by clearing the clutter from your automobile, a drawer, your living room, or maybe your bathroom cabinet. You'll quickly begin to experience the benefits of living with less. And you'll know what to do when you finally arrive at the seemingly impossible areas in your home.

A few years back, I ran a marathon. It was the fulfillment of a life dream. I had always wanted to run one as an exercise in self-discipline and focus, but the challenge always seemed too difficult. How would I ever run 26.2 miles? What about that stretch of mile 20 to mile 26? Where would I find the mental strength to run through the "wall" as I neared the end?

The fear of running 26.2 miles kept me from even trying. That was, until I picked up a book titled, *Run Your First Marathon*. While I ultimately found conversations with other marathon runners to be a bit more helpful in my training, this book by Grete Waitz provided me with all the motivation to get started. Specifically, it was the training guide that motivated me the most. It read something like this:

—Day 1: Run 1 mile.
—Day 2: Rest.
—Day 3: Run 1.5 miles.
—Day 4: Rest.

I knew I could run one mile—that was an easy step. I even knew I could probably run two miles—and that would get me all the way through almost the whole first week. I found great motivation in this training plan.

Suddenly, I stopped worrying so much about miles 20-26.2 and I just stayed focused on accomplishing what I knew I could accomplish. Ultimately, the lessons I learned while running 1, 2, and 5 miles prepared me to run 10, 12, 14. The lessons I learned running 10, 12, and 14 miles prepared me to run 18, 20, and eventually 26.2.

So go ahead. Start your decluttering journey with the easiest step. Pick one drawer or one lived-in area (living room, bedroom) of your home. Leave your toughest questions for mile 20. You'll get there when you are ready.

The Simple Guide to a Clutterfree Home.

I've lived most of my adult life in a cluttered home. Closets were full, drawers wouldn't shut, things weren't put away, and unfinished projects could be found in most rooms.

That is, unless somebody was coming over. Then, the entire family would pitch in to make sure the house was presentable. Looking back, the problem with clutter wasn't that we didn't notice or care. The problem was we could never get ahead of the mess or ever seem to develop a system that would keep our home clutterfree.

But that is no longer the case. Today, almost every room in our home rests in a state of order—free from the life-robbing presence of physical clutter. Over the past several years, we have found a system of habits that work very well for our family. I am perfectly confident you can do the same—no matter how far away from clutterfree your home may seem.

Consider implementing the four steps found in this chapter to keep your home clutterfree.

1. Believe it is possible. Most of us know it is entirely possible to live in a clutterfree environment. I imagine that is what attracts you to this guide. You are just looking for some extra help to get there.

But some of you are not so sure. Your house has been cluttered for so long, you have given up all hope of ever living any other way. For you, the first step to living in a clutterfree home is to take heart and believe it is entirely possible. Realize you will never get there if you do not resolve in your mind you can accomplish it. So find some hope and take one small step. Then, take another...and another...and another.

2. Remove the excess. Our homes are full of things. Clutter begins to appear most prominently when we own too much stuff. Conversely, the fewer items we own, the easier it is to keep clutter at a minimum. The first (and most important) step in keeping your home clutterfree is to remove the excessive possessions that are stealing your life, time, and energy.

In your process of removing the excess, it can be helpful to find a working definition of clutter to aid you in this step. Clutter is a) too much stuff in too small a space; b) anything you no longer use or love; or c) anything that leads to a feeling of disorganization. With that as a guiding filter, slowly move from room to room, removing everything that fits the definition above.

In some cases, this step is easy:

—Junk drawers full of unneeded items.
—Closets full of clothes no longer worn.
—Decorations no longer meaningful and/or outdated.

In other cases, this step will take more time and intentionality:

—Large projects such as the garage, basement, or attic.
—Sentimental items that have collected over the years.
—Books.

Other times it can even be more difficult. But the process is always the same: easy steps first and declutter one area at a time. Regardless of the specific room or project, start with the small and easy projects first. Build up small victories. Then, after the small victories have been won, you'll find extra motivation to begin tackling the harder cases of clutter in your home.

If you still do not feel fully capable of removing the excess possessions from your home, find encouragement in an intermediate step. For example, put the items you can't quite part with in a cardboard box out of sight with a date on it. Getting rid of unnecessary possessions is essential, but it doesn't have to be a race.

3. Implement habits to manage your clutter. For most of my life, I thought the key to defeating clutter was found here. Just organize, clean, and organize again. But I was wrong. Because I had not taken the time to remove the excess in full (or in part), I could never get ahead of the clutter in my home. There were just too many things in too small a space—no matter what system we tried to implement. As a result, healthy clutter-clearing habits never had the opportunity to emerge. So do not skip the step of de-owning, it is vitally important. The more energy you put in removing the excess, the easier it will be to find and develop habits to better manage the things you keep.

Once you have cleared the excess, you will be able to better discover which habits keep your living space free of clutter. And, once you experience the freedom and stress-free life of living clutterfree, you will find these habits easier to embrace.

Some of these habits will recur daily:

—Cleaning the kitchen after each meal.

—Returning daily-use items.

—Fully-completing projects around the house.

—Developing an evening routine.

Some of these habits will center on specific locations that serve as clutter collection sites in your home. For us, our kitchen counter typically collects items (mail, schoolwork) during the day, our living room sees a high-volume of traffic each day, and one of the bedrooms in our home finds itself a bit messier than the others. Each of these specific locations require extra effort and energy than the others.

Some habits will center on seasonal needs:

—The changing of the seasons.

—The need to purge after holidays and/or birthdays.

—Life changes (birth of a child, new employment).

Over the years, we have found clutter attracts clutter. Once it begins to collect, it requires intentional action to clear it away. Develop for your family healthy habits today to manage the daily use of the things in your home. Once identified, you'll find them much easier to implement.

4. Slow the accumulation of possessions. To live is to consume. It cannot be avoided—especially in our society and culture. But if the influx of possessions into our homes can be slowed, clutter can be managed efficiently.

To slow the accumulation of things in our homes, we need to change our mindset that assumes more is better and begin evaluating our purchases differently. Realize your purchases cost far more than the price on the sticker. Each one will also require time, energy, and effort once they enter your home. Before making a purchase, begin asking yourself some tough questions.

Is this item really needed? Do I have a place to store it?

How much extra work will this possession add to my life? Am I buying it for the right reasons?

This thought-process is not designed to keep you from making purchases ever again—at least, it's not supposed to. To live is to consume. These questions are designed to bring greater intentionality into your life. They increase the awareness that some purchases take more from our life than they offer. They help you know the difference. And slow the accumulation of clutter.

Again, it is possible to live in a clutterfree home. With these four simple steps, you'll be well on your way. From somebody who has lived both, I can quickly attest that once you begin to enjoy the physical and mental freedom that accompanies clutterfree living, you'll make extra effort to ensure your home does not slip back into the home it used to be.

The Simple Joy of One.

Once you are on your way developing decluttering habits, consider taking your efforts to an even deeper level. Experiment a bit.

When we first started decluttering our home, we started noticing a troubling trend: duplicates. In fact, we owned duplicates of nearly everything: linens, jackets, tennis shoes, candles, televisions, even duplicate remote controls to control the same TV! We began to quickly realize we had bought into thinking that went like this, "If owning one of something is nice, owning more will be even better." But we were wrong.

I have begun to intentionally embrace a new philosophy: *there is a peaceful joy found in the presence of owning one.* There are actually a number of benefits to it.

We own only our favorite of every object. We take better care of our belongings. We regularly use each of our possessions. We experience less clutter in our home. We create the opportunity to own higher quality items. We find more capacity to help others with our excess. And we experience increased intentionality in our purchases and possessions.

If one is sufficient, more is not necessarily better.

This principle can be applied to almost any item we own: One television. One set of bedding. One coat. One belt. One spatula. One...

Conversely, there is little need to own duplicate items that serve the same purpose.

I invite you to test out the principle in your own life. Choose a safe place to start (perhaps decide to wear only one sweatshirt for the next 10 days). And experiment with the idea of owning only one. If you find the practice to be burdensome, you can end your experiment early. But, on the other hand, if you find freedom in your new habit, look for other places to apply it.

Surely, the practical implications of this principle will vary from household to household. Its opportunity will play out differently in your home than mine.

The simple joy of owning one has too quickly been forgotten. It is time we remember its simple beauty—and live less cluttered lives because of it.

[5]
Including Your Kids in the Journey

"The rules for parents are but three... love, limit,
and let them be." —Elaine M. Ward

Children add joy, purpose, and fulfillment to our lives.
They bring us smiles, optimism, and cheerful attitudes.
Given the chance, **they** will teach **us** valuable lessons about
life.

Certainly, growing children (physically, socially,
intellectually, and emotionally) have added a new dimension
to our minimalist journey, but I wouldn't want it any other
way. In fact, some of the most important lessons about life
and minimalism have been learned by watching my
children.

One neighborhood friend is worth more than a basement
full of toys. My two kids spend countless hours with their
neighborhood friends running from yard to yard, playing
tag, catching bugs, or swinging on swings. They can spend
every afternoon and evening together without being bored.
But take them away from their friends for one Saturday at
home with their toys and boredom almost immediately sets
in. The joy of playing alone in a roomful of toys quickly

fades—no matter how expensive the toys were to buy.

Lesson Learned: Relationships with others are always more exciting and fulfilling than possessions.

Clothes are not worn to impress others. My elementary school-aged son has two requirements for his clothing: 1) that he can get them dirty and 2) that he won't get too hot. He has never worn a shirt to impress a girl or a pair of slacks to impress his teacher. (He has worn a shirt and slacks because his parents asked him to, but that's a different subject). I don't think the idea of trying to impress others by wearing the latest fashions has ever crossed his mind. He feels no pressure to conform or impress. And thus, he's simply content with a clean T-shirt and shorts.

Lesson Learned: Wear clothing for its usefulness rather than as an attempt to impress others.

Life's pains are healed best by a hug and a kiss, not new toys. My daughter has fallen down often (as most kids do). When she skins her knee, she only wants one thing—her mommy to pick her up, give her a kiss, and tell her that everything is going to be okay. She doesn't ask for a new toy —she only desires love and security. She has found the antidote to pain and wouldn't trade it for anything else.

Lesson Learned: Don't look towards "things" to soothe the pain we encounter in life. Instead, seek love, acceptance, and security.

Fancy possessions and character are completely unrelated. I love helping in my daughter's second grade classroom because early elementary may be the only place left on earth where labels don't exist. At age 7, everyone is accepted and everyone plays with everyone else. Each person starts the day on an equal footing. Nobody is prejudged by the house they live in or the clothes they wear. Oh, that our world would begin to resemble a first-grade classroom.

Lesson Learned: Judge people by their hearts and character, not by the meaningless externals of life.

Too many toys in a box only get in the way of the good ones. A funny thing happens after holidays. A mountain of new toys enter our children's lives. The toys are initially met with incredible excitement. However, after two or three days, they are pushed to the side as our kids return to the tried-and-true toys they had been playing with long before the holiday ever occurred. The new toys we thought would make them happier, don't. Instead, they just start to get in the way.

Lesson Learned: We often think that material possessions will bring lasting excitement into our life, but most of the time they just end up getting in the way.

The more toys you play with, the more time you spend cleaning them up. Because we clean up every night before bed (well, almost every night), our kids understand this pretty simple equation. The more toys we pull out of the closet, the more time we spend cleaning them up. And, the less time we spend actually enjoying them.

Lesson Learned: The more possessions we own, the more of our time is required to care for them.

A hike in the woods beats a new video game any day.

Video games simply can not compete with the graphics, the full-sensory experience, or the relationship of a family walk through the woods. Never have, never will. And for that matter, nothing else produced on television can compete either.

Lesson Learned: Turn off the television. Go outside. Live life, don't just watch it.

Perhaps children are in this world because we as grown-ups have so much left to relearn.

Teaching Simplicity to Your Kids.

Clutterfree with kids requires a little more effort, a little more thoughtfulness, and a lot more patience. As you embark (or continue) on this journey, there are several practical steps you should not neglect.

Explain your decision. Your children are thinking human beings. Therefore, no matter their age (our son and daughter were only 5 and 2 at the time), sit down and explain your decision to them—include the reasons why you are choosing to embrace simplicity and the benefits you are hoping to receive from it. And because teenagers typically jump to far-reaching conclusions, assure them your decision does not mean you are no longer going to buy anything...it just means you are going to intentionally think through your purchases in the future.

Begin organizing your possessions first. Remove your excess personal belongings first and your shared family belongings second. It would be unfair to ask your child/ teenager to thoroughly adopt a clutterfree lifestyle until you have done it personally. Also remember, you will learn valuable lessons when you remove your personal clutter— valuable lessons that will put you in a better place to help your son or daughter navigate their journey.

Remove the physical items they do not use first. Clutterfree is about paring down to only the essentials. It is about removing the things in our life we do not need so we can better focus on the things we do. And while most homes are filled with things that are not needed, they are also filled with things that are not even used. Start there. You can begin by removing the clothes they no longer wear, the toys they no longer play with, and the other things they no longer use. That's an easy first step. As you begin there and talk them through the process, they may begin to naturally start asking themselves, "How much of this other stuff do I really need anyway?"

Focus on the positives. As you begin to see the benefits of simplicity in the life of your children/teenagers, point them out and focus on them. Just because you are observant enough to notice them, doesn't mean they see it quite as readily as you. Does their room appear tidier? Do they spend less time cleaning? Is it easier to find things? Can you notice less stress or less distraction? Are you more relaxed as a parent? Encourage each other with the positive benefits you notice.

Treat them to fun experiences. One benefit of living

clutterfree is that you spend less money on material goods and have more time on your hands—so you may have some extra disposable income and the time to do something with it. Use it to create fun, exciting, family experiences. Do something new that everyone will enjoy. Take a trip to the beach, the amusement park, or a weekend in the city. You don't need to spend all of your newfound savings on one trip (especially if you are trying to get out of debt in the process), but a practical experience that highlights the benefits of your decision can go a long way in helping your children understand it better.

Choose your purchases carefully going forward. You will still need to buy things going forward. Children will outgrow their clothes, their toys, their school supplies, and their sporting goods. They are not going to stop growing and developing. You are absolutely still going to buy things going forward—you are just going to put more thought into your purchases than you did in the past. Replace "Do I want this?" with "Do I need this?" And help your son or daughter ask the same question. It's one of the most important lessons they will ever learn.

Be patient. Be patient with your family. Offer them plenty of time to adjust to simpler living rather than being pushed into it. This new lifestyle is one that needs to be believed in and adopted. Show them plenty of patience. After all, if it took you 20-30+ years to finally adopt a lifestyle of living with less, it would be foolish to assume they will fully adopt it in 30 minutes—or even 30 days.

But again, let me assure you. Simplicity is completely achievable and beneficial for you and your family. It is worth the investment. You'll love it!

Section 2
Discover New Habits

[6]
Toys

Stories of Change: *Sara K., Washington D.C.*

Sara has always been averse to clutter. From the time she and her husband brought home their now-2-year-old son, Sara was determined not to change her clutterfree approach —especially now that there was a child in the house. But as a rolling stone gathers moss, so a toddler gathers toys. And eventually, they had to instill a few new habits to ensure his playthings didn't take over the house.

Their first habit is periodic minimizing. Every few months, Sara digs through the toy box and sets aside for donation those items that have fallen out of favor.

Their second habit started because their condo is small. At just 800 square feet, it doesn't have a separate playroom. Their son's toys live in the open-plan living/dining room, so tidying up twice a day became necessary. Eventually, this habit became their son's first chore. Before nap time and bedtime, he dutifully replaces his books on his bookshelf, his toys in their baskets, and parks his cars against the wall— learning valuable life lessons along the way.

The third habit is frequent library and park visits. Amazon

tempts all of us with regular emails promoting its most popular books and toys, but Sara works hard to remind herself she has a well-stocked library and several playgrounds within walking distance. They check out a few new books every week and return them, immediately followed by fun on the big (communal) toys that stay at the park.

Clutterfree has always been Sara's preference, but the introduction of children into her family and home has required her to become more intentional. While there have been numerous moments of frustration, she has discovered with just a little thought and energy, clutterfree with kids is entirely possible. It just takes a little more thought sometimes.

Change Your Thinking.

Toys are not merely playthings. Toys form the building blocks for our children's future. They teach our children about the world and about themselves. They send messages and communicate values. And thus, wise parents think about what foundation is being laid by the toys that are given to their kids.

Intentional parents also think about the number of toys that children are given. While most toy rooms and bedrooms today are filled to the ceiling with toys, intentional parents learn to limit the number of toys that kids have.

They understand that fewer toys will actually benefit their children in the long-term.

Kids learn to be more creative. Too many toys prevent kids from fully developing their gift of imagination. Two German public health workers (Strick and Schubert) conducted an experiment in which the authors convinced a kindergarten classroom to remove all of their toys for three months. Although boredom set in during the initial stages of the experiment, the children soon began to use their basic surroundings to invent games and use imagination in their playing.[9]

Kids develop longer attention spans. When too many toys are introduced into a child's life, their attention span will begin to suffer. A child will rarely learn to fully appreciate the toy in front of them when there are countless options still remaining on the shelf behind them.

Kids establish better social skills. Children with fewer toys learn how to develop interpersonal relationships with other kids and adults. They learn the give and take of a good conversation. And studies have attributed positive childhood friendships to a greater chance of success academically and in social situations during adulthood.[10]

Kids learn to take better care of things. When kids have too many toys, they will naturally take less care of them. They will not learn to value them if there is always a replacement ready at hand. If you have a child who is constantly damaging their toys, just take a bunch away. He will quickly learn.

Kids develop a greater love for reading, writing, and art. Fewer toys allows your children to love books, music, coloring, and painting. A love for art will help them better appreciate beauty, emotion, and communication in their world.

Kids become more resourceful. In education, students aren't just given the answer to a problem; they are given the tools to find the answer. In entertainment and play, the same principle can be applied. Fewer toys causes children to become resourceful by solving problems with only the materials at hand. And resourcefulness is a gift with unlimited potential.

Kids argue with each other less. This may seem counterintuitive. Many parents believe that more toys will result in less fighting because there are more options available. However, the opposite is true far too often. Siblings argue about toys. Every time we introduce a new toy into the relationship, we give them another reason to establish their "territory" among the others. On the other hand, siblings with fewer toys are forced to share, collaborate, and work together.

Kids learn perseverance. Children who have too many toys give up too quickly. If they have a toy that they can't figure out, it will quickly be discarded for the sake of a different, easier one. Kids with fewer toys learn perseverance, patience, and determination.

Kids become less selfish. Kids who get everything they want believe they can have everything they want. This attitude will quickly lead to an unhealthy (and unbecoming) lifestyle.

Kids experience more of nature. Children who do not have a basement full of toys are more apt to play outside and develop a deep appreciation for nature. They are also more likely to be involved in physical exercise which results in healthier and happier bodies.

Kids learn to find satisfaction outside of the toy store. True joy and contentment will never be found in the aisles of a toy store. Kids who have been raised to think the answer to their desires can be bought with money have believed the same lie as their parents. Instead, children need encouragement to live countercultural lives finding joy in things that truly last.

Kids live in a cleaner, tidier home. If you have children, you know that toy clutter can quickly take over an entire home. Fewer toys results in a less-cluttered, cleaner, healthier home.

I'm not anti-toy. I'm just pro-child. So do your child a favor today and limit their number of toys. (Just don't tell them you got the idea from me.)

Discover New Habits.

Over the past several years, we have taken intentional steps to minimize the number of toys in our home. Sometimes we feel like we are winning the battle, other days we feel like we are losing. Perhaps you can relate.

But regardless of the day-to-day feelings, we have

discovered several very practical tips to help minimize the number of toys in our home. Hopefully, you will find encouragement in them to begin winning the battle against toy clutter.

To be fair, the exact "ideal number" of toys will vary from family to family (if there even is one). But hopefully, each of these tips will be helpful to those of you who know the ideal number is less than you have today.

Be convinced that less is better. As with any clutterfree (or simplifying) project, it always begins with a heartfelt belief that less is better and desirable. I'm assuming if you have picked up this book and read past the first several chapters, you already believe this to be true.

Fewer toys is different than no toys. Toys can be educational and play an important role in a child's development. Just to be clear, I'm not advocating no toys, I'm arguing for less.

Analyze your own motivation for purchasing toys. Most children don't buy toys for themselves—somebody else does. If there are too many toys in your home, start with yourself. Why are there so many toys in your home? A healthy look at your own motivations may go a long way in solving this problem.

Choose quality over quantity. You and your children will benefit more from toys that are chosen for their quality (in workmanship) and purpose (playability) than for their sheer quantity. And just like everything else in life, too many toys will always distract from the truly important ones.

Purge often. Most likely, you need to make a clean-sweep of your children's toys right now. Removing the "low-hanging fruit" (toys that are no longer used) is a great place to start and shouldn't take too long. Put the clean, unused toys in boxes and donate them to a medical center, nonprofit organization, local church, homeless shelter, orphanage, school, or Goodwill. Simply discard the dirty or broken ones. Then, stay on top of the clutter by purging on a regular basis and going beyond the low-hanging fruit.

Set a confined, physical space for toys. Whether it is a container, a shelving unit, or a closet, set a confined physical space for your children's toys. Once the space is full, there is no room to add more toys. Help your children understand this principle by clearly marking the boundaries. If they want to add (think holidays and birthdays), they'll need to remove first.

Limit your purchasing with a budget. If you budget for other categories in your life (groceries, clothing, entertainment), you already understand how this principle helps keep your spending and consumption in check. If you don't, start today by setting a monthly/yearly budget for toys. Enforcing a predetermined budget amount will help in limiting your toy purchases.

Don't give in to fads. Just like clockwork, toy companies will generate a new "toy-fad" every few months by artificially generating a cultural buzz. If done well, this artificial buzz will become mainstream in the culture and no longer feel artificial. But it is, and it will always pass. You don't need to give in just because every other parent does.

Keep a healthy, realistic attitude toward toy companies and toy stores. They may tell you that their main goal is to help or educate your child, but most often, they are driven by their bottom line. This does not mean there is no educational value in the toy they are marketing, it just means we need to be mindful of their motivation and decipher their claims better because of it.

Avoid duplicate toys. Instead, require siblings to learn the invaluable life lessons of sharing, generosity, cooperation, and compromise.

Find a local toy library. Consider borrowing toys rather than purchasing them.

Watch less television. Marketers are brilliant at shaping the desires of men and women, young and old. Now, imagine giving them hours each day to shape your children's minds too—and you'll quickly realize that you don't stand a chance.

Don't give in to temper-tantrums at the store. Every time you give in to a temper-tantrum at the store just to avoid a scene, you embolden your child to do it again. They quickly learn how to manipulate you. Don't worry about the scene that is taking place in public. Wise parents in the store will respect you for not giving in—and the foolish ones will learn a valuable lesson.

Equip your children to make wise choices. Involve your kids in the purging process. Help them make decisions about which toys should stay and which should go. This will serve them well into adulthood. After all, don't you wish your parents had forced you to learn that skill?

Teach them to value other activities. Although all kids have natural tendencies towards certain endeavors, expand their mind by regularly introducing them to new activities that don't revolve around toys.

Limit your toys too. Kids will always learn more from example than words. If your life is caught up always needing to own the latest fashion, technology, or product on the market, theirs will be too. It would be unreasonable to expect anything less.

Keeping fewer toys will never be easy. It will always require thought and intentionality. But it will always result in your children learning to value who they are more than what they have. And that always makes it worth the effort.

Free Your Home.

If you were to make an honest assessment of your home's toy stash, would you say you own too many, too little, or just the right amount?

When you first began assessing the number of toys in your home, which type of toy popped into your head as overflowing (trucks, dolls, crafts, large plastic toys)? Is this a good area to minimize first?

How many rooms in your home have toys stored in them? Is

it possible to consolidate and remove the toys entirely from one room (or even two)?

What type of physical boundaries have been established in your home to contain your child's toys? Is there a natural one you could begin using (closet, cupboard, wall)? Could your child thrive with an even smaller boundary?

Did any unhealthy toy-buying motivations begin to surface in your mind during this chapter? What steps can be taken to eliminate them?

[7]
Clothes

Stories of Change: *Ciara C., Dublin, Ireland*

Ciara spends her days with busy professionals at work advising them about efficient ways to manage email, tasks, and priorities. But being organized doesn't come naturally to her—it's something she has had to work at. In doing so, it has helped her focus and achieve many successes in life.

But home organization has always been even more of a struggle for her. She lives in a small open plan townhouse with three boys, her husband, and dog. She struggles to keep order, the calm control of her working environment evaporating as she walks through the door. But she says things are getting better; little by little she has introduced ways and means of staying calm and keeping the house clutterfree. Her latest obstacle has been to take control of the children's clothes.

Her younger two boys are now eight and nine and old enough to take on more responsibility looking after their own belongings. So why was she finding sweatshirts, socks, and football shorts all over the house every day of the week —not to mention the clothes she would find beside the shower or beside the bed in a pile that looked like a body has just evaporated from them?

She knew something needed to change.

To curb the momentum, she and her husband came up with two ideas. The first was to label the children's drawers and the second was to do a clean sweep each night before bed time. Everyone must start at the front door and work their way through each room collecting their belongings as they go.

The labeling has been a huge success; the labels go on shelves, drawers, and cupboards and the kids know exactly where their clothes need to go. She has observed a sense of pride from the kids when the work is done. The clean sweep habit is coming up against a little resistance but with time she believes they will see the benefits of less work during the day. Overall the results have been very positive.   A clutterfree space and more importantly, peace and harmony —at least, for a little while anyway.

Change Your Thinking.

Consider for just a moment how your life would look different if you owned fewer clothes. You would have more disposable income. You would have more time to live your life. Mornings would feature less stress. Your closets would be well-organized and clutterfree. Packing for trips/vacations would take less time. Laundry days would be easier (not necessarily less, but definitely easier).

Unfortunately, instead of enjoying the benefits of owning fewer clothes, most of us buy into the lie that more is better. Because we do, we accumulate more and more clothing each season. We are convinced that new clothes will make us more fashionable, more popular, and more joyful. Unfortunately, they just end up getting in the way.

Consider going a different route with your life. Try owning fewer clothes. You may be surprised at how much you enjoy the freedom it brings.

I can remember where I was when I first heard about Project 333—little did I know how it would eventually cause me to rethink my wardrobe in every imaginable way. I was visiting family in Omaha, NE, when one of my friends mentioned she was picking out her clothes for *Project 333*.

I was intrigued. Then, the next thing I knew, I was in.

Project 333, founded by Courtney Carver, is a 3-month long experiment in personal fashion. The rules are simple: Wear only 33 articles of clothing for 3 months. All clothing, accessories, jewelry, outerwear and shoes count towards your number—exceptions include wedding ring, underwear, sleep wear, in-home lounge wear, and workout clothing. Clothing that no longer fits or becomes in poor condition may be replaced during the time period.[11]

Initially, I decided to try it because the project sounded both challenging and reasonable, the community seemed encouraging, and pushing personal limits is almost always beneficial. The project began on October 1 and concluded on December 31.

To be fair, I broke the rules twice during the experiment (once during a trip to Phoenix when I wore an uncounted pair of shorts and once during an Ugly Sweater Christmas party when I wore an uncounted ugly sweater). Other than that, I was able to stick to the rules of 33 articles of clothing with only minimal adjustments to my weekly routine.

I discovered the project was not about forced suffering. It was about setting boundaries. It was about experimenting with life inside them. Ultimately, it was about improving our lives through them.

Indeed, boundaries offer numerous benefits.

Boundaries keep us restrained. Artificial boundaries can keep us in check when our natural self-control does not. Over the years, I had amassed a closet full of clothes—far more than I ever needed. Looking back, I am embarrassed at the amount of time, money, energy, and attention devoted to my clothes.

Boundaries force our values. When you are challenged to pare down your clothing to 33 items, you are forced to identify which items are absolutely necessary. You are forced to single out the most important, most versatile, and most loved items. You are required to identify the absolutely most valuable things in your closet.

Boundaries promote creativity. Orson Welles said, *"The enemy of art is the absence of limitations."* Limiting your clothing items to 33 items for 3 months forces art. Limiting your wardrobe does not rob you of personal style—it causes you to find it.

Boundaries bring freedom. This may sound contradictory and depending on the exact boundaries, it may be. But in the example of clothing, I found great freedom in the boundary provided. So much so, that even though I've finished the project, my closet still holds only 33 items. It has been years since the challenge, and I have not added anything to it.

It is refreshing to look inside your closet and see only clothes you love. Getting ready in the morning is less time-consuming. Laundry is easier. I've saved countless dollars since the original experiment. The experiment has granted me more time, energy, and money—and if that's not the definition of freedom, I don't know what is.

The true value of boundaries reaches far beyond our closets. It begins to spill into how we decorate our homes, the toys we buy for our children, the amount of clutter in our kitchens, and how we choose to spend our time, money, and energy.

In many ways, it caused me to rethink clothing—and opened up a brand-new world in the process. As a result, you'll discover the value of boundaries (both physical and mental) promoted as a major theme throughout this book.

Discover New Habits.

Whether you are hoping to minimize your wardrobe to the absolute minimum or just paring down the amount of clothing in your child's closet or drawers, the steps are the same. Now, while it may appear easier to declutter your child's closet (or your spouse's), I strongly recommend you begin on your own side of the closet. Not only will it serve as a good example (especially if fashion is important to your daughter—which it is for mine), but the lessons you learn and motivation you find keeping your own closet clutterfree will be helpful as you begin decluttering theirs.

I have included a helpful list of 12 practical steps for you to consider. All of them are important, but some will come easier to you than others. These are the same steps we have used in our home.

Admit you own too much clothing. That's all you really need to get started.

Embrace the idea of wearing fewer colors. Most of us already have a few favorite colors we wear anyway—usually because we like the way we look in them. Choosing to intentionally wear fewer colors means less accessories (shoes, belts, jewelry, handbags, etc.). It almost makes too much sense not to try.

Embrace the idea of one. When one can be enough, embrace it—one swimsuit, one winter coat, one black belt, one pair of black shoes, one handbag—insert your own based on your lifestyle, climate, and kid's activities.

Donate, sell, recycle, discard. Depending on the size of one's existing wardrobe, an initial paring down won't take long. You can typically cut down your wardrobe by over 25% by simply asking, "If I was out shopping right this second, would I buy this?" If the answer is no, throw it into a donate, sell, or recycle pile.

Donate, sell, discard some more. Removing the clothes you no longer wear or like is easy. Removing the clothes you don't really need can be a tougher choice. Turn around all the hangers in your child's closet. When an item is worn, return it with the hanger facing the normal direction. After the season is over, remove every article of clothing that wasn't worn. That should help get you started on a second round of paring down.

Bless others with still-wearable clothing. Kids grow quickly. As a result, they often grow out of clothes before they are fully worn. If they do, be quick to donate those clothes to another family. You can do far more good (and find far more joy) by giving them to another rather than keeping them for yourselves. The temptation may be to keep them for future little brothers or sisters. But, there is only a small chance that the gender and season will line up exactly the same anyway (especially in seasonal climates). If another family can use them today, you'll reduce your clutter by giving them away—and the act of generosity will likely be returned in the future.

Impose an arbitrary moratorium on shopping. For many, clothes shopping is just a habit—and habit always takes over for inattention. To break the cycle of purchasing and discarding (the average American throws away 68 pounds of textiles each year[12]), set a self-imposed buying freeze. I recommend 90 days. If given enough time, this simple exercise in self-discipline will change your view of your clothing and the stores that produce, market, and sell them.

Do not be led astray by changing fashion. Henry David Thoreau once said, *"Every generation laughs at the old fashions, but follows religiously the new."* It is important to understand fashion trends are artificially manufactured by the fashion industry to sell more product. Don't be duped in your closet or your child's. Find a fashion you enjoy that never goes out of style. Refuse to embrace new, artificially manufactured trends. The only thing they produce is more clutter.

Purchase quality over quantity. Buy clothing you truly love—even if it costs more. If you stock your closet full of things you love, you will have less desire to add to it.

Bring your intentionality with you to the sale racks. Sales can and should be used to help you get a better price on clothing your growing child will need in the future (for example: a coat for next winter or a new swimsuit for next summer). Unfortunately, because of their nature, most sale racks end up persuading us to purchase something we don't actually need. This doesn't mean they need to be avoided, it just means we need to approach them with very specific intentionality.

Remind yourself of the lessons you are teaching your kids. Especially as they get older, kids will want/desire certain articles of clothing based on the influence of their peers. These items are not always wrong to purchase. But if they are trying to impress others with the clothes on their back, they are going about it the wrong way. Teach your children to impress with their character, not with their clothes. After all, character never goes out of style.

The average American household spends $1700 on clothing and services each year.[13] Given that fact, even small changes in the size of our wardrobe can have long-lasting financial and life-giving effects.

Free Your Home.

Without looking, guess what percentage of the clothes in your closet are worn regularly? Now, go take a look and see if you were right—literally separating the hangers if you need to. Was the actual percentage higher or lower? Try the same experiment with your child's clothing.

When it comes to your kids' clothing, would there be benefit to owning less? Which benefits come to mind?

Can you walk into your child's room right now and remove 10 articles of clothing that are not needed? Can you remove 15? (Depending on your child's age, you may need to include them in this experiment).

Which store's sales and discounts tempt you into purchasing the most clothing that does not get worn frequently? How can you approach shopping in that store with greater intentionality?

[8]
Artwork

Stories of Change: *Siouxzy P., Essex, England*

Siouxzy has always been conscious of how "stuff" can bring stress into her life, while creating art makes her feel calm, more free.

When she had her first son 8 years ago, she encouraged him to create, paint, write, and draw, but until recently, she felt pressured to keep every piece of work he'd ever produced. It is not an untypical response for any parent—especially for an artist by nature. In fact, it was even in her heritage. She still owned every school book from her childhood—her parents had kept them all. At this point in her life, the thought of sorting through them was almost too burdensome.

Recently, Siouxzy decided she did not want to burden her children with that weight. Instead, she wanted to teach them the joy of letting go. Now, as a general guideline in her home, once an item of art has been displayed in the house, it goes into recycling. If the piece is particularly special or something he's very proud of, her son keeps a folder with those most precious pieces. When the folder gets too full, he sorts through it and chooses what has to go. This requires regular and intentional purging.

Through the process, she has learned how something that may feel too sentimental to let go of in the present, often years later does not hold the same importance. But in an attempt to be better safe than sorry, she invested in a cheap scanner to digitize some pieces she thought they might want to remember. She has found she is far more likely to reminisce by looking through digital files than by dragging a box down from the loft.

Most importantly, Siouxzy believes it teaches her children how to work through what is important and what is not—even from a young age. As she says, "Those types of life skills are essential for a productive and meaningful life."

Change Your Thinking.

My daughter is an artist—in every traditional sense of the word. She loves writing, drawing, coloring, painting, stickers, and every imaginable type of craft. Left unchecked, she will quickly fill drawers, cupboards, and counter space with her many creations. Not only is creating a passion of hers, but it is a skill in which she has displayed considerable natural talent. Balancing her love of art and my love of a clutterfree home has resulted in new outpourings of both patience and compromise.

Amidst her ever-increasing love of art and resulting collections, I have made an important realization. A realization that caused me to forever rethink the relationship between clutterfree and works of art. But it took a visit to a friend's house for this important life lesson to emerge.

I have a friend with a bookcase in her living room. It has four shelves. On the shelves sit 36 books, 11 figurines, 24 photos, 2 souvenir coffee mugs, various snow globes, flower arrangements, vases, and candles.

Can you picture it in your mind? Good.

Now, with that picture in the back of your mind, consider that living clutterfree is not just the removal of unnecessary physical possessions. It is also the intentional promotion of the things we value most. It is about deciding what is most important in your life and removing the things that distract you from it.

Which directs us back to the mental image you have formed of my friend's bookcase and eventually my daughter's artwork. When I look at my friend's bookcase, I ask myself, "What is it that she values most? What is most important to her?" Is it books? Family? Coffee? Snowglobes? You see, I can't tell by simply looking at her bookcase—it is crowded with too many things that are less important. And my attention is stolen from the most important.

Imagine curating items for display in a museum. Museum organizers work diligently to find and place only the most important pieces on their museum walls. Whether it be art, history, sport, or technology, these pieces communicate a specific story. If you include too many items, the story is lost. For that reason, only the most important (or most representative) pieces are allowed on display.

One benefit of simple and clutterfree is you are able to *visibly* declare what is most important to you and what you are most proud of in your life. Wherever you are sitting right now, look around. What does the living space around you communicate? If a stranger walked in, what would they identify is most important? Would they be right? Or have the less important things crowded out the most important?

As I consider my daughter's love for art, I have begun to realize the important truth that keeping everything is the same as keeping nothing. When everything is kept or when everything is displayed, nothing is allowed to take precedence—the less important always steals attention from the most important. In this way, it is not unloving to curate our child's creations. On the contrary, it is vital in order to allow the most precious pieces to speak the loudest (as Siouxzy attested above).

Discover New Habits.

We have found kids' artwork (and paperwork) to be a never-ending stream of input. As I mentioned, I am okay with that. I do not want to diminish my daughter's love and appreciation for creating new and beautiful things. These are important skills for her to embrace and develop throughout life. She ought to be allowed to experiment and create.

But I do want to keep our home clutterfree. Not just for our sake, but so her creativity can flourish even more. I want to reinforce her love for art by proudly displaying the work she is most proud of—the type of work that encourages her and us to develop her gift even more.

Using the steps below, we have been able to strike a valuable balance.

Adopt a museum mentality. Become a curator of your child's artwork. You don't make a great museum by putting all the art in the world into a single room. In fact, what makes a museum great is the stuff that's not on the walls—it's the stuff you leave out that matters. Not everything your child creates is a masterpiece. Not everything they create needs to be displayed and/or stored. Keep the best. And then, challenge them to create even more of their very best.

Hang it/Display it. Some of the most treasured pieces of art in our home were handmade by someone we love. Displaying art created by someone you love adds special meaning and special value—far more than buying something on clearance at a department store. Use some of your child's work on your walls and shelves. Again, use only their best. You can embrace a rotation system if there are a number of pieces worthy of display.

Set storage boundaries. One way to help with the curating process is to establish storage boundaries. My daughter has one plastic bin that holds all of her artwork. When the bin fills, we declutter. We include her in the process asking her to decide which items to keep and which items to remove (our oversight helps her keep an assortment of pieces that displays her versatility and growth).

Capture it with photos. When you do remove pieces, some may be more difficult than others. This may indicate a need to expand your boundaries...or maybe a single camera will be sufficient instead. Taking a photo of your child's artwork is advantageous on many levels. A digital photo preserves the art longer than the actual piece and causes no physical clutter in the process. Having your child hold each item will serve as a chronological marker of the pieces that are removed.

Create a memorable souvenir. With the use of a camera or scanner, even people with limited Internet and/or artistic prowess can create beautiful, lasting, and clutterfree souvenirs using any number of Internet websites. Snapfish is one example we have used numerous times. For $20 (sometimes even less), parents can create high-quality hardbound books using digital files of their child's work. Once the work is displayed in this format, parting with the original pieces becomes much easier.

Give some away. Grandparents love seeing and experiencing the artwork of their grandchildren. Pass some along. This can be done with the actual pieces if curated properly (no need to overwhelm them with too many pieces). Or make a Snapfish book of the best pieces just for their coffee table.

If you parent a creative, celebrate! Artists add special beauty and thoughtfulness to our world. Embrace it. Encourage it. And curate. In the long run, both of you will benefit from the intentional effort.

Free Your Home.

What type of art is your child's favorite to create? How have you encouraged this development in him/her?

Closing your eyes, can you picture 3-4 of your son/daughter's best and most meaningful creations? Where are they now? Is there a place they can be displayed prominently? Can they replace an existing piece of art that carries less significance?

Have physical boundaries been set for the collection and storage of your child's artwork? If not, what would work best in your home? If so, are you keeping the boundaries or do they need to be revisited/curated?

What is the last art museum you have taken your child to experience? Is it time to go again? Or maybe for the first time?

[9]
Sentimental Items

Stories of Change: *Michele N., United Kingdom*

In 1990, Michele and her family downsized from a three bedroom house to a 24-foot RV to begin traveling and exploring. At the time, her family consisted of her husband, two children, three dogs, and a cat. Her kids were both under 12 years old.

Michele knew the hardest thing for her family to part with would be sentimental possessions such as photographs, old love letters, and gifts from those who were no longer living. Yet, they knew the confines of the RV required them to make tough decisions. Some of the items were passed on to family members, some to close friends who would treasure them, and the rest were either sold or given to charity/thrift shops. They found motivation realizing they didn't really need to keep the sentimental possessions. Michele recalls knowing they still had the memories—and it was the memories that held the real value.

For the two young children, there were items they had treasured since birth, but Michele suggested they sell what they felt was not deserving of the little space they had available. In exchange, they could have the money and spend it as they desired. Both boys bargained hard at the weekly market stall. Michele remembers being proud as they made surprisingly mature choices.

By giving them the power of choice and a clear allocation of space, the boys felt empowered to welcome the change. Additionally, Michele looks backs and sees the process as influential in the formation of their own value system.

Today, they are both adults, running their own businesses with children of their own. And both grown men cite the downsizing operation as a pivotal moment in discovering both a flexible approach to life and the confidence to navigate it successfully.

Change Your Thinking.

Less is different than none. One thing I hope you have noticed throughout the chapters of this book is that owning nothing is not the goal of clutterfree. Intentionality is. Our lives can stand for so much more than the possessions we accumulate. It is a shame so much of our potential is sidetracked because of them.

Of course, not all of our possessions are purchased, some were handed down to us. And in some cases, these can be the most difficult items to declutter—especially when the objects hold important memories. Whether the memories relate to our grandparents or our kids, we can quickly become emotionally attached to these possessions because of the memories they prompt.

Unfortunately, too often, these precious sentimental objects are stored in boxes in the garage, attic, or basement. We enjoy owning the objects because of the memories they prompt, but find their day-to-day value pretty limited. As a result, they are often stored out-of-sight and only discovered during deep cleanings, a relocation, or a specific desire to travel down memory lane.

But there is a better way to handle these sentimental objects. If we owned fewer of them, they could become more accessible, more visible, and more significant. Similar to the artwork mentioned in the previous chapter, it is easier to display one object that defined your grandmother's life than it is to display seven.

Indeed, it is important to change our thinking on this issue. Less is different than none. And less is far better than too many.

Discover New Habits.

How then, do we get rid of the stuff that means so much and evokes so much emotion in the name of simplicity? There are several ways to simplify the sentimental. As we review them here, notice how each concept includes focusing on what is important and choosing to honor your story.

Do not start here. Quite frequently, especially for those predisposed to sentimentality, memory-invoking items are the most difficult to consider parting with. Whether it be toys from our childhood we hope to pass on or tokens of memory from our child's young life, the idea of removing the items in our home that tell a story has caused many a parent to completely reject the notion of owning less. But remember, there is no need to begin removing the most difficult things first. You can start easy. Build up momentum and motivation for these more difficult decisions. When you get there, you will have developed a helpful filter for making these choices. This book is written to be a helpful resource guide. But if you are starting here and think it is just too difficult, you may want to choose an easier chapter first.

Consider the benefits. We have said much about the benefits of owning less. But in this specific case, revisit some of them. What might be some benefits of owning fewer sentimental souvenirs?

Our homes would be less cluttered. We'd be less tied to the past, more free to move forward. By owning less, we would draw more attention to the most important. It would place less pressure on our children to keep the things important to us. Our minds would be more free to create new memories in the future.

Choose an arbitrary boundary. One of the reasons we keep so many sentimental items in our homes is because there is no boundary to force our hand in making a decision. As a result, more and more boxes get moved into the attic to store this ever-increasing collection. Instead, set an arbitrary boundary: one box, one drawer, or one shelf. Setting this boundary will help you separate the *most* important from the *kinda* important. And you'll find it to be easier than you thought.

Share the love. Rather than keeping your objects in a box, display them for others to see. These items are important to you. They have helped to define who you are and what your values are. If you have done the first steps well, this step will be easier and will make perfect sense. After all, a box full of memories stashed in the basement is far less meaningful than 3-4 specific items displayed proudly in your home.

Make it useful. Did you save the china that your parents received on their wedding day or a special necklace that was passed down to you? Why not use it? Donate your everyday plates and eat off the dishes that mean so much. Wear the memorable piece of jewelry every day instead of waiting for a special occasion or worse, forgetting about it completely.

Photos, photos, photos. If there are items you are struggling to remove because of the memories attached, take a picture before letting them go. Preserve the memories inspired by stuff through photography. The memories are not in the object—the memories are inside you. The photo will serve as a useful prompt when needed. Again, you could use a web-service such as Snapfish to make photo books of the items.

Put it in the cloud. If you have been saving printed photographs, documents, receipts, and other paperwork for years, it might be time to digitize your docs. Sort through it all and toss the trash. Scan the rest or hire someone to do it for you, and organize in folders. From there, back it up through Dropbox.

Tell your story. The most powerful thing you can offer is your story. As you simplify your life, you will come to the realization that the most sentimental things aren't things at all. They are the stories of the people and the places you love. Write about the things you love, instead of holding onto them. Start a family blog or keep a personal journal. Your words may start out describing your mother's watch, but turn into a beautiful story about an afternoon the two of you spent together.

Free Your Home.

Would you typically classify yourself as a sentimental person? Why or why not? Is there a deeper answer than "It's just the way I am?"

What specific type of sentimental items do you struggle parting with?

Has your collection of sentimental items (whether yours or your children's) become burdensome in any way?

What is a good first step to begin decluttering the sentimental things in your home?

Collections

Stories of Change: *Robyn D., Omaha, NE*

Robyn's journey to clutterfree began not too long ago. While her husband saves very few things (power cords for various machines being tops on the list), Robyn came from a long line of savers. Her family members have been known to save everything including old Cool Whip containers and baby food jars, boxes sitting in their basements from 20-year-old moves, and all the packaging for any and everything ever purchased—just in case.

It was out of this environment she emerged, and while Robyn had become much better over the years—thanks in no small part to the influence of her husband—she was still most definitely a saver.

One spring afternoon, she was trying to find the perfect yarn to use for knitting up a hat, when she stopped and looked around. Robyn noticed she was surrounded—by yarn, knitting needles, knitting notions and books, and that didn't even begin to describe the rest of the clutter around her!

With just one sobering glance around the office/craft

room, Robyn realized something had to change. There was just too much stuff in her house. She declared then and there she would learn to balance minimalism and knitting.

In the months following her decision, Robyn gave away almost half of her yarn stash and committed to knit through the remainder of it within the next twelve months. She began the difficult process of paring down the rest of what she owned as well, working towards the goal of owning as little as possible.

She immediately found owning less freed her up to do what she truly loved—not just knit, but parent her children as well. Robyn found an amazing community of minimalists on the internet, people who live similarly, sharing their lives, and inspiring her do the same.

It's been a slow process for Robyn, but a fun one. More importantly, it's been life-changing.

Change Your Thinking.

When I was young, I collected baseball cards. (I also collected *Garbage Pail Kid* cards for a short summer, though I prefer not to mention it often). Over the years, I spent countless hours riding my bike to the convenience store, spent countless dollars I earned from chores around the house, and probably added countless cavities from the sugary bubble-gum in the packages. Even today, decades later, I can look back on those days and that collection with great fondness.

Though I did not realize it at the time, I was actually strengthening my brain and my mind with those card collections. I only knew I loved baseball and sorting the cards by team, player, or value. But additionally, child psychologists tell me I was developing my brain to organize in different ways, recognize patterns, and notice unique characteristics. The act of collecting and sorting was building and strengthening nerve connections as well as encouraging creativity. It was the equivalent to a physical workout for my mind. Go figure.

It is important for us as parents to recognize these positive aspects. Often times, especially among those who value simplicity and order, parents begin to see these childhood collections as clutter or a nuisance—or even worse, habits that might develop into hoarder tendencies. But in reality, in almost every case, these collections are quite normal and helpful. They promote patience, presentation skills, goal-setting, and displaying pride in ownership. While the desire to collect is more apparent in some kids than others, the benefits include social, organizational, and intellectual growth.

The thought pattern for us as parents then ought not to be on removing these collections, but instead, focusing on how to manage them effectively.

Discover New Habits.

All the benefits being understood, there is still opportunity to emphasize the importance of intentionality, mindfulness, and distraction—in all areas of life. A child who begins collecting seashells one day, but switches to rocks the next, and feathers after that will find little progress in their hobby. While there is room for experimentation in collecting, consistency should also be valued.

Likewise, there are other life skills we should teach our kids by helping to organize their collections in a clutterfree way.

Help kids understand the idea of opportunity cost. Opportunity cost is a business term that represents the loss of potential gain from other alternatives when one alternative is chosen. In nonbusiness terms, it simply refers to the fact that every decision we make has consequences. Saying "yes" to anything (a purchase, an appointment, an emotion) requires us to say "no" to everything else—that is the opportunity cost. If your child is a collector, use the habit as a helpful means to teach him/her the importance of opportunity cost. (For example, collecting sea shells means less opportunity for building sand castles).

Understand the difference between consumer-driven collections and hobby collections. Advertisers make their living by creating impulses and encouraging kids (and parents) to follow them. Marketing to kids is highly advantageous because they can change focus so quickly (notice any Beanie Babies on the department store shelf recently?). Similar to decluttering toys, keep your eyes open to fads manufactured by Madison Avenue. They go by quickly—and the costs can add up even faster.

Find comfort in the existence of boundaries. Your child's collection boundaries will vary wildly. A rock collection will most certainly take up more space than a collection of state quarters, for example. Additionally, each of our homes provide a differing amount of space available for kid's collections. Choose a space that is appropriate for your home, your children, and their collections. And curate to value the best. In our home, my daughter uses her bottom drawer for collections (currently rocks).

Purge items as preferences change. As kids get older, their tastes and passions evolve. This is fully natural and expected. What may have been fun to collect over the past two years may not be as enjoyable as they age and mature. If the collection holds no monetary value, purging these items can be relatively painless. If there are financial concerns (either in current worth or sunk costs), the decision may require more thought and investment. But taking the time to do so will prove quite beneficial for both you and your child. It will provide the physical space for a new collection and the mental space to fully invest into the new one.

Free Your Home.

Were you a collector as a child? If so, what did you collect? And what memories are associated with it?

Is your child similar to you or different in this regard? Do they love to collect? If so, what? Do they skip around from one collection to another or do they stay focused on just one?

Is their current hobby influenced by advertising? Or did it arise organically? How did you reach this conclusion?

What boundaries are currently in place for your child's collections? Do they need to be adjusted? Has this conversation spurred any other strategic ideas to change your home?

[11]
Screens

Stories of Change: Kendra K., *Corpus Christi, TX*

Kendra's home was one completely oriented around the television. And she would be the first to tell you her family spent a lot of time watching it. Like many American families, their evenings and weekends were planned around television schedules and filled with whatever was the hot programming of the day.

That was, until May of this past year. During the spring, they moved to a new home in Corpus Christi, TX. While preparing to move their belongings and dogs, Kendra determined it was a perfect opportunity to further simplify their home and lives. After all, moving houses requires every possession to be handled multiple times and decluttering unneeded items arises naturally during the process.

While talking over the opportunity to simplify, Kendra challenged her family to cancel their cable subscription—or at least, not renew it in the new home. It was going to be a big change for their family, but she thought it was worth the effort.

She recalls some difficulty. At first, her husband and

teenage daughter complained—often times reminding her all that they were missing. But within a few weeks, a new normal began to emerge.

The importance of television in their family time began to fade. Without television as an option, the family began gravitating towards reading or being outside together. The television was no longer the focal point of their home. It was no longer feeding their urges. And the absence of advertisements was allowing consumeristic tendencies to fade.

They still own a television set and use Apple TV to watch a few of their favorite shows. But their life is no longer dictated by screen time. They have discovered a better use of their time (and the $120/month savings is nice as well). At this point, Kendra can't imagine why they'd subscribe to that old life again.

Change Your Thinking.

The statistics concerning the television watching habits of children are really quite unbelievable.

According to the Kaiser Family Foundation, kids under age 6 watch an average of about 2 hours of screen media a day, primarily TV and videos or DVDs. Kids and teens 8 to 18 years spend nearly 4 hours a day in front of a TV screen and almost 2 additional hours on the computer (outside of schoolwork) and playing video games. Counting all media outlets, 8-18 year-olds devote an average of 7 hours and 38 minutes to using entertainment media across a typical day.[14]

As you can probably guess, the effects of television on children are not good. Children who watch too much television: 1) carry a much higher risk of childhood obesity, 2) are more likely to display aggressive behavior, 3) are more likely to engage in "risky behaviors" when they get older, 4) have less energy, 5) have a harder time in school, and 6) are more-exposed to commercials, advertisements, and propaganda.[15]

We live in a world of increasing media consumption. Ignoring its impact is no longer possible. Additionally, prohibiting it completely is probably no longer wise. As with most things in life, moderation is key.

Discover New Habits.

To help inspire parents to find moderation in their child's life toward screen time (TV, video games, computers, iPods, etc), I recommend a number of helpful tips and tricks. And while each of them are tried-and-true methods used in our home and others, there is no need to incorporate all 12 at once. Instead, start with the habits that will be most helpful for you and your family. You can always add more in the future if necessary.

Set the example. Sorry to start with the toughest one, but there is nowhere else to start. Children will always gravitate toward the modeled behaviors of their parents. If they see you reading a book, they are more likely to read. And, if they see you watching television, they are likely to join you.

Be the parent. It is your job to encourage healthy behaviors and limit unhealthy ones—sometimes this means making unpopular decisions. Make these tough decisions for your children. Always go the next step of explaining why you have made the decision—this will help them follow through and someday choose it for themselves.

Set limited viewing times. If you are not going to turn off the television completely, choose the appropriate television viewing windows for your kids. It is much easier to limit their viewing habit if they understand that they can only watch one show in the morning and one show after school (as just an example).

Encourage other activities. Provide the necessary resources (books to read, board games, art supplies, and/or sporting equipment).

Play with your kids. Get down on the floor with your kids and pick up a doll, truck, or ball. It takes intentionality and selfless love when they are 6. But when they turn 13, you'll be glad you did.

Be involved in their lives. For many parents, it is just easier to turn on the television than to actually be involved in the lives of their children. But those intimate life details are required for successful parenting. So observe, listen, ask, and parent.

Cut your cable / remove your television completely. If you want a sure-fire way to limit your child's television viewing habits, cut your cable/satellite television feed (or remove your television completely). It will change your family's life overnight (it changed ours). Oh, by the way, it will positively impact your checkbook too.

Observe your child's behavioral changes. Television has an immediate impact on your child's behavior. After too much television/video games, my children get irritable, aggressive, selfish, and impatient. I can tell almost the moment I walk in the door. Be on the look-out for these behavioral changes. When you start to notice them yourself, you'll be less inclined to put your kids in front of the screen.

Don't worry if they miss out on parts of the conversation. Your child's friends will talk about television. They will compare notes about cartoons, Disney Channel, or prime-time programming. You will think that you are depriving your child of friendships because they can not join in on those parts of the conversation (I'm speaking from experience). But don't worry. You will have successfully prepared your child to enter into far deeper, richer conversations than the most recent television reality series episode.

Value family meals and car rides. About two-thirds (64%) of young people say the TV is usually on during meals.[16] That's too bad because your family's richest conversations will always take place during meals and in the car. Value those times with your kids. Don't let the TV steal them from you.

No TV's in bedrooms. Not your kids' rooms. And not yours either.

Find your mantra. A mantra is a sound, word, or group of words that are considered capable of creating transformation. While the words may not be magic in themselves, the consistent use of them can be. Every parent should have them and use them effectively. My "too-much television" mantra goes like this, "There's been too much screen time in this family." And every time my kids hear me say it, they know what it means...they know we are about to do something together as a family.

Limiting your child's screen time may seem like an impossible chore or it may seem like a battle too difficult to fight. But it is worth fighting. Limiting your child's screen input will have a positive impact on your journey to clutterfree (most of those advertisements are brainwashing us anyway).

Implementing just a few steps right away will help you implement the others. Television viewing is a momentum-gathering behavior. The more you do it, the more compelled you are to do it (advertisements have that effect on viewers). But the opposite is also true. The more you turn it off, the easier it becomes to turn off. You've just got to start somewhere.

Free Your Home.

Are you surprised by the statistics above? As you rethink the past week in your home, how many hours per day have your children spent engaged with a screen? Are you content with that amount or sense a change is necessary?

Do you notice any change in the behavior of your children when the television has been on for an extended (or even short) period of time?

Are family meals and car rides valued in your family to the extent of turning off the television and other media? Would you like it to be? If so, go for it (it is your family).

Is there any mindless television watching in your own life that can be replaced with more profitable pursuits? If so, what mantra might you incorporate into your mind to shift your focus?

[12]
Photos

Stories of Change: *Trina C., Lincoln, NE*

Trina C. from the Heartland found herself overwhelmed with her family's photos. She remembers what started as a mild interest in capturing the everyday, grew stronger with the birth of her daughter. It somehow became her duty to not let a moment go by that wasn't documented as their baby grew.

She didn't notice it right away, but it became more of a burden than a joy. She didn't have time to sort or organize the hundreds of photos, let alone print or store them. Even backing them up was a chore she avoided, and learned its importance the hard way. Her daughter was six-months old when their laptop died, taking with it all the photos from the start of their family—not even the computer professionals could access the files from the retired hard drive.

Even after losing all of their personal photos, the shift to decide taking (and keeping) fewer photos happened slowly. Trina realized beyond the time spent managing hundreds, even thousands, of photos she had taken, the camera kept her from being fully in the moment.

She eventually accepted that taking a handful of photos each year was more than enough to look through and enjoy and pass on as her kids grew. With time, she became more intentional about leaving the camera behind. When she enjoyed moments with her family thinking, "I want to lock this in memory," she did just that. She took in the smells and the feels and the sounds—those details that the camera usually diluted for her.

As a bonus, Trina found that intentionality with the photos she took allowed her to focus on quality versus quantity—the photos she captured and saved were beautiful pieces worth preserving.

Change Your Thinking.

As parents, we've all been there. We bring the camera to the school choir concert, the baseball game, or the family vacation. Point, click. Point, click. Point, click. By the end of the game/concert, we've snapped 15-20 pictures; but depending on our skill, maybe 4-5 are quality pictures worth saving. The others are marked by closed eyes, open mouths, or fingers over the flash. But when we get home and plug the digital card into the computer, we still select "upload all photos." After all, the kids need to get into bed...or we just need a chance to sit down and catch our breath.

Unfortunately, the photos never get sorted. And the next time a special event happens, we repeat the process (if you can't tell, I'm speaking from experience here).

Eventually, our computers fill up with hundreds (or even thousands) of photos never to be thought of again. That is, until, we need that one specific photo for the school video collage. At this point, you can forget about finding anything quickly—even if your computer's photo software organizes them well.

It is important for us to change our thinking on photographs. There will never be a time in the present or the future when we will need/use every photo we have ever taken. Instead, whether we are discussing a baby book, a high school graduation, or a wedding video, we will always only choose the best ones. And we will save ourselves plenty of time in the future—and clutter in the present—by keeping only the best and removing the rest.

Discover New Habits.

If you have the photography gene, I offer no promise that becoming clutterfree with your photos will be easy. In fact, it will probably be one of the most time-consuming sections of this book. But I encourage you to push through and gain victory in this area discovering new habits along the way. It will pay incredible dividends in the future.

Choose your software. When it comes to digital photos, know your software options. There are plenty that will help you in this area. If you use a Macintosh computer, iPhoto will do the trick and should already be installed on your laptop or desktop. If you do not use Macintosh or do not like iPhoto, there are a number of photo organizers you can purchase or download for free. Among the free options, Picasa works well. Among the paid, I recommend Adobe Photoshop Elements as an inexpensive option. I do all my editing in Photoshop Elements.

Sort. Whether we are discussing physical photos or digital photos, the first step to find sanity is to develop a sorting system that works for you. The easiest way (and often times the most convenient for perusing later) is to sort your photos by date. Most digital organizers use this system as the default. Until you get your physical photos scanned into a computer where they are safer and last longer, this is an ideal sorting system for them too.

Value Originality. Quality photos vary in scene, angle, backgrounds, and facial expressions. Be sure to keep a varied assortment of photos: funny faces, smiling faces, and serious faces. Keep action shots and still shots, groups and individuals. The best photos are not the ones that match a certain criteria or formula, the best photos are the ones that jump off the page (or screen) when you first see them. Keep those—regardless of the type.

Purge. Purging your photos ruthlessly will result in a collection that is easy to review and enjoyable to relive—just imagine the enjoyment found in going through your photos when each one is high-quality and memory-packed. The best time to purge photos is immediately when you upload them into the computer because the reason you took the photos is freshest in your mind. If any photos did not turn out because of faulty flashes, poor focus, or mistiming, delete them permanently. If you took photos of the same pose several times, only keep the best. And unless you are a nature photographer, keep a minimal amount of photos without faces.

Rate. I recommend designating some of your top photos within your software with a top rating (5-stars for example). Save this designation for only your absolute favorite photos —those photos you just can't get out of your mind. These then, can quickly be recalled when you are looking for just a few really good photos.

Store your photos "in the cloud." Most photo organizing experts (and photographers) will advise you to use cloud-based photo storage for your photos. These would include popular websites such as Flickr and Picasa or using an Internet-based storage solution such as Dropbox or iCloud. First, storing your photos elsewhere acts as security for your memories if your computer is ever lost, stolen, or destroyed. Second, storing your photos in the cloud allows them to be accessed anywhere. And third, storing photos on your personal computer uses memory and can slow down your computer.

Stay ahead of the game going forward. Certainly, as you can probably imagine, this will take some intentional effort at the very beginning. Do yourself a favor and stay ahead of the game moving forward. Certainly, take as many pictures as possible. But staying committed to keeping only the best will result in great dividends in the future.

Of course, if the project is simply too overwhelming for you and the expense is of little concern, you could always hire a professional organizer to do the project for you. Some even specialize in sorting digital photography.

Free Your Home.

Do you have the photography bug?

Without looking, can you name your 2-3 favorite photos of your child? Do you know where/how to locate the original if you need it?

Are you content with your current system for organizing digital photos? What about physical photos?

From the list above, what is the most important step you could take in the next week to get started?

Do you use any cloud-based storage for your favorite photos? Is that a step you need to make time for sooner rather than later?

[13]
Gifts

Stories of Change: *Lisa M., Dallas, TX*

After Lisa had 2 children before the age of 20, she set off to acquire the things she deemed necessary to achieve a middle class lifestyle. Her priority was to establish and own a home filled with items heralding her success. Deep down, her desire was to "look nothing like a stereotypical teenage mother."

She began working two jobs at a time—and this continued for many years.

Toys, clothes, furniture, and decorations were bought and then promptly given away when she flippantly chose a new theme for her house. Sometimes, more than once/year she would change everything: furniture and curtains included.

She was making good money and would hire maid services to clean and organize all the stuff in her home while she went off to earn more money to buy more stuff.

Lisa recalls buying gifts for her kids almost daily. She remembers it getting to the point where she would come home from work, walk in the front door, and be greeted everyday with, "Hi Mom, what did you bring us today?"

Now, looking back, Lisa regrets trying to buy happiness. It was clearly not working.

One day, when her children were at school, the house burned to the ground due to an electrical fire. With not enough lessons learned, Lisa quickly replaced the house and its contents and proceeded to spend the next several years repeating the cycle.

But then, Lisa's father was diagnosed with advanced Parkinson's disease. He was a collector—even a hoarder of electronics and machinery. He developed this habit throughout life and spent much of his time buying items at auctions and swap meets and storing them in his house and his garage—anywhere he could find the room for them.

As he became sicker and unable to do the things he used to, Lisa traveled to his home 1,100 miles away multiple times. With the help of her brother, they cleaned out several tons of his purchases from the basement and garages. Safety was now the first priority for his living space—and this way of living was not safe.

The process caused Lisa to begin reflecting on her own life. He had spent so much time and energy with his hobby and yet, it was all removed in the blink of an eye as if it had no importance. The money wasted and time invested seemed sad, almost heartbreaking.

She was forced to reflect on her own habits, the time she had wasted, and how much of her children's childhood had been wasted buying things only to maintain them at their expense!

Lisa set out on a life transformation. Over the next 6 months, she gave away more than 70% of her stuff. Almost immediately, she began feeling more peaceful, more calm, and centered on more important pursuits.

She even plans to sell her house and get something smaller so she can travel more easily. She'd like nothing more than to spend her money and time making valuable memories with her now-grown kids instead of leaving them a bunch of useless material things.

Change Your Thinking.

Gift-giving is a tradition as old as time itself. I'm even more than positive cave drawings signify the practice of gift-giving among the earliest human beings (though a scientific source is still needed). Either way, it has been around a long time.

Yet, gift-giving is a tradition birthed by numerous motivations. Gifts can be given for the purpose of expressing love, showing appreciation, gaining favor, smoothing over a disagreement, or even manipulating for personal gain. Because of these many varied motivations, our approach to decluttering gifts can sometimes be difficult to implement—especially if the motivations behind gift-giving are selfish in nature.

Before considering how to declutter gifts, it is important to remind ourselves of these motivations so we can recognize them and proceed appropriately.

Personally, I respect gift-giving as a love language and do not want to rob my family members of that simple joy. If this is their motivation, I prefer quality over quantity, needs over wants, experiences over products, and provide gift wish-lists whenever possible. For the kids, we reevaluate toy boxes and closet space a few months after the holidays/birthdays to determine if there are items (new or old) to remove. The philosophy is simple, straightforward, and easy to manage.

On the other hand, if the motivation behind gift-giving is manipulative in nature, I have other opinions. Gifts given with an ulterior motive or a hidden agenda are much less appreciated. These can be difficult to recognize at first, but over time, givers with these manipulative habits begin to identify themselves. I have less hesitancy in speaking up to those gift-givers—and this does not have to be done in a confrontational manner, it can still be accomplished with respect and tact.

The most difficult gift-giver to handle is the one who should be motivated by love, but is motivated by selfish gain instead. Sometimes, even they may not realize the strings they attach to the gifts they offer. It is important to be aware and assertive in these circumstances. Ask the giver if they are expecting anything in return for the gift. Often times, forcing them to audibly declare "no" will be a helpful step for both them and you. If the problem persists, it is absolutely within your right to not accept a gift. If this is the only way for the giver to recognize the severity of their problem, you are actually giving them a gift by saying no.

Discover New Habits.

For the sake of this conversation, let's seek to address the genuine gift-giving process. Holidays, birthdays, and special circumstances seem to stack on top of one another. Given our culture's propensity to commercialize any and every festival and celebration, the receiving of gifts and the subsequent clutter is most certainly on your mind (and in your home).

How can we create space to both humbly accept gifts and remain clutterfree?

Begin with fewer possessions. I remember my daughter celebrating her 3rd birthday shortly after our decision to minimize. Princesses were everywhere—on the decorations, the paper products, the cake, and on her presents. Everywhere I looked I saw princesses...and my daughter smiling. She couldn't get enough! Every card and gift with a princess brought a smile to her face and a cheer of "princesses!" Her joy brought me joy.

Looking back on the day as we were taking the new princess toys to the basement toy room, it occurs to me one benefit of living clutterfree is it provides "room to add." Because we had kept our kids' toys down to a minimum through regular sorting and purging, there was room in our basement for new princess toys. Conversely, if the toy room was already stuffed full of toys, there would be no room for my daughter's new treasures.

Make your gift requests known early. Though it does not always work out this way, gift-givers should desire to match their gifts with the receiver's desire. Sometimes gifts are given with the expectation it will be appreciated even though not requested—and sometimes they are right. But creating gift lists and providing them to family members well in advance of holidays and celebrations can be a very helpful tool in limiting the clutter collection. Work hard to provide a wide range of gift ideas varying in prices. Again, follow this formula: request quality over quantity, needs over wants, and experiences over products.

Be patient with your family. If living with less is a new pursuit for you, do not expect everyone else in your family to understand the first time around (especially if you are known for going through various phases in the past). Eventually, years down the road, they will begin to understand this is a lifestyle you are seeking to embrace for the long term and their gift-giving habits will likely evolve.

Humbly accept they may indeed have a good idea. Pride is always costly. It prevents us from seeing important life changes and other people's points of view (among other things). This is important to remember when accepting gifts —especially from thoughtful gift-givers. When accepting gifts, embrace the idea that they may indeed know something that will add value into your life and benefit you in the long run. Be open to receiving their gifts and input. It would be foolish and proud for us to assume we know all the good things that could be added to our lives.

Purge guilt-free. It may take some time for you and your kids to sort out which holiday gifts add value to your home and which only add clutter. With the kids, it can often take months to determine which toys are a passing fad and which will become truly loved. Give it some time. But as the value of the gifts begin to reveal themselves, purge guilt-free. The gifts were given to you or your children (ideally with no strings attached). And, if they will find more use to be given to someone else, then please don't hesitate to give them away. Rare is the gift-giver who wants their gift to be a burden on you or your home.

Reciprocate your request. You hope, desire, and expect other people to give gifts that align with your desires. Return the sentiment when you give gifts to others. Just because you make a desperate plea for experiences over products does not mean your brother, sister, father, or mother is requesting the same. If they would like new shoes, consider buying them new shoes. If they make it clear they desire a department store gift card for their birthday, at the very least, consider giving them a department store gift card. Giving gifts is an opportunity to show your love and appreciation. You can make your case for anti-consumerism at a different time.

Winston Churchill once wrote, *"We make a living by what we get. But we make a life by what we give."* There are countless benefits to living with less. One of the greatest benefits is the newfound freedom to pursue generosity with our money, our time, and talents. May we, as those who seek to live intentional lives, break free from the selfish tendencies of consumerism. And instead, choose to err on the side of generosity. May it be expressed in our gift-giving—and may we be generous in our gift-receiving as well.

Free Your Home.

What is your current philosophy on giving gifts to your children (number, budget, tradition of opening)? Can you track its roots? Were you raised this way or have you developed it on your own? How did you get here?

Do the gift-givers in your family do so with proper intent? Do they genuinely have your best in mind or are they motivated by selfish desires? How has this influenced your understanding of and ability to receive gifts?

Are there gifts you have received from others that are proving difficult for you to remove even though you don't want them? What thinking is causing you to keep it? Can it be replaced with a healthier mindset instead?

Are there any specific ways you can replace possessions with experiences at your next upcoming gift-exchange opportunity?

[14]
Packing

Stories of Change: *Kellie M., Nairobi, Kenya*

For most of her life, Kellie was a heavy packer. Because she disliked unfamiliarity, she tended to travel with as much of her daily use stuff as possible hoping to make the new place feel like home.

One time, for an overnight stay at a friend's house, she recalls packing 3 outfits, 2 pairs of shoes, soap, cosmetics, and more—eventually needing a mid-sized suitcase for the trip. Things only got worse when she became a mother.

Her first trip with her daughter required 4 hours of packing. By the end, the luggage filled so much of her station wagon, there was no space for anyone else but her and her daughter's car seat. Every other spot in the roomy car (including the space below the car seat) was full! She chuckles remembering now that her destination was not some remote part of Kenya, but her own mother's house.

But everything changed for Kellie while visiting her sister. While enjoying a meal together, Kellie's sister decided to have her two kids travel back with Kellie to stay at their mom's house for a few days so the kids could play together.

To Kellie's shock, her sister took less than 10 minutes to pack up a small bag of clothes for the two toddlers. No spoons. No special cups. Just clothes, diapers, and baby oil in a small travel bag.

That is when Kellie realized she didn't need to travel with all the stuff she typically brought.

A bit later when preparing for a trip out of town, she stuck to only the essentials which translated to one backpack and one small plastic container for her utensils. The same station wagon that did not have space for even one extra person the last time ended up carrying 3 adults, a toddler, and all their luggage for a one week vacation.

Rather than feeling panicked and inadequate when they arrived, the holiday was nothing but good fun. Kellie says she'll never return to over-packing for trips. Not now that she has realized how refreshing it is to pack light.

Change Your Thinking.

There is something very freeing about travel. It offers opportunity to experience new things, meet new people, and learn valuable lessons. Unfortunately, many of us unnecessarily burden our travels by carrying too much stuff with us. Including myself.

We used to be heavy packers, always stuffing our suitcases and bags to the point where the zippers were about to burst.

In fact, on one trip home for Christmas, we had packed our four-door vehicle so full that we had to take some of our presents out of their cardboard packaging just to make them fit in the car for our drive home. Not a pretty sight. And an even worse way to live.

As a family with young children, we thought it was the best way to travel—that it brought security. After all, with our bags and trunk-full, we were prepared for any unexpected emergency or opportunity that would arise during our trips.

What we failed to realize is the process of transporting so much stuff with us was not adding joy, security, or freedom to our trips. It was doing the exact opposite. It was making our trips burdensome and weighty.

It required extra time to pack, unpack, load, and unload again. Packing heavy was not reducing the amount of stress involved in our trips as we assumed it would. It was creating more stress. It was important to bring the necessities, but trying to imagine every possible unforeseen scenario that might arise during our trip was burdensome and far less helpful than we imagined.

Today, we pack much lighter. On weekend trips, our family of four easily fits into one suitcase. On extended trips (week or longer), we easily fit into two suitcases.

This has brought many advantages. Packing has become easier and less time-consuming. Loading and unloading happens in one trip. Settling in to new accommodations (hotel/family) takes far less time than ever before. Moving about airports is less stressful .Not to mention, the savings on checked bag fees.

We are freer. We are lighter. Travel has become more enjoyable since learning to pack lightly.

Discover New Habits.

To begin traveling light and learning to pack clutterfree, I'll offer a few practical tips we have learned to adopt as we transformed our habits in this area.

While you will find benefit in each of them, there is no need to adopt each of these every time in order to reduce packing clutter. You may find it is easier at first to embrace one or two or three that work best for you and your family. Or, you may even find freedom in testing out a few tips during a short trip with the family before adopting them for a longer time away. Give them a good test run. You'll see what I mean.

Set limits. If you travel by air, you are already accustomed to doing this. Most airlines limit the weight of your luggage to 50lb per piece. But have you ever considered the possibility of self-imposing limits on space? You could try limiting your family's luggage to only one piece of luggage or two if necessary. If your family members pack for themselves, establish your own weight restrictions. The limits, if properly set, will force and foster increased intentionality in your choices.

Pack versatility. Travel with lightweight, layerable clothing. Choose dark clothing that gets less dirty. And pack matching separates that can easily be converted into a number of different outfits. In our experience, 2-3 pairs of shoes (sometimes less) can cover almost any situation that will arise. And kids' shorts and T-shirts can easily be substituted for sleepwear. Think multipurpose and avoid packing single-purpose items.

Digitize when possible. The internet is a valuable tool. If you own a smartphone, get to know the various opportunities that can help you reduce your physical clutter on trips. For starters, a simple map application can eliminate paper clutter. Current technology has almost limitless functionalities. Your electronic device can eliminate the need to pack itineraries, tickets, books, movies, reservations, and receipts. If you haven't already, spend some time researching what the options may be. After all, you are already paying for most of them.

Don't allow cultural stereotypes to fuel overpacking. Sometimes, our overpacking is foolishly fueled by cultural expectations that we put on ourselves. For example, I used to think that I needed to pack a certain number of apparel items just so I could avoid wearing the same thing more than once. This over-packing was based on an incorrect cultural stereotype. Namely, that successful people didn't wear the same clothes two days in a row. Because my transition into minimalism was such a drastic change, I had a wide opening (and newfound desire) to pack lightly and wear the same pants/shorts 2-3 days in a row. And guess what? I don't think anyone has even noticed the change. My packing is now in line with my vacation goals. I travel to visit family and see new sites, not to impress people with my vast wardrobe folded into a suitcase.

Limit the Extras. Travel with fewer amenities. Your home has become a stockpile for all sorts of comforts and luxuries. Once we have brought so many little comforts into our lives, it can be difficult to picture life without them. But you were fine before and you will be fine again—especially for only a short time. Pack fewer toiletries, accessories, and emergency supplies. Evaluate each item. Is it really necessary for me to pack this? Could I try living without it for one weekend? If so, try. You can almost always go buy the item during your trip if you really did need it with you.

Free Your Home.

Are you an overpacker? Isn't it freeing to just admit it?

In what ways did the "Change your Thinking" section above cause you to rethink packing lightly? What specific benefits would surface in your life if you chose to pack less?

Are there any items that regularly get packed in your luggage that never get used on your trips? Is it an object that can be removed from your packing list next time?

When is your next upcoming trip? What is one way you can limit the physical space available to you for packing? Can you take one less piece of luggage? Can you take a smaller piece instead of a larger one?

Schedules

Stories of Change: *Jana B., Aberdeen, SD*

Jana always knew she wanted to limit the amount of activities her kids would be allowed to be in. She would attest to seeing families running around all day long, eating meals in the car on the way to their next event, getting home late in the evening, and forcing their exhausted children to quickly get their homework done because it was already bedtime. And then get up early the next day just to do it all again.

This is not the kind of lifestyle she wanted for her family.

This past summer, partly because of her self-professed procrastination and partly because of scheduling conflicts, none of her 3 children were involved in any activities. Normally, they would have been in swimming lessons or tennis lessons enjoying their typical one activity at a time guideline. But this summer would have to be different.

Interestingly, Jana recalls this summer being their most enjoyable season since the kids were born. All summer long, the family was free to do whatever they wanted every day.

They made it a goal to visit every park in their town at least once during the summer. If they woke up and wanted to visit the library, they did it. If the weather was nice, they'd visit the pool. If dad got home early and they wanted a family bike ride, they'd go for a ride or walk.

No schedule, no pressure, just whatever moved them that day. The family began a tradition of playing baseball in the backyard together almost every night after supper. Jana recounts each of the kids learning more about baseball from the private, one-on-one coaching from her husband than they would have ever learned from a summer program anyway. Plus, the memories will last a lifetime!

Jana has no misconceptions about the reality of this schedule getting more difficult as the kids get older. But for this past summer, she wouldn't change a thing. It further reinforced her resolve to think hard about the number of activities her kids are involved in. As she has learned to say, "Family time will never take a backseat to another activity."

Change Your Thinking.

Intentional parents desire to help their kids learn skills, gain confidence, grow in character, find interests, and experience new opportunities. When they are young, we desire to give them every opportunity to discover what they love and where they will succeed.

For many of us, this results in busy schedules. We are often presented the opportunity by living in a community that offers countless options. We feel compelled by the fear that our kids will fall behind. We are guilted into the life by relatives, friends, or neighbors. Unfortunately, there seems to be a little voice inside each us calling us to impress other parents by the success of our children. As the philosopher Ernest Becker might say, *"We exalt our children into the position of our own 'immortality symbol'."*[17]

Somewhere along the way, childhood activities became less about the goals outlined above and more about trying to keep up with everyone else. Or even worse, they became less about our kids and more about ourselves. Though we would never care to admit it, in some cases, busy schedules became less about improving our kids' lives and more about us proving our value to other parents—as if busy, successful kids is a badge of honor we could wear on our sleeves to parties and social outings.

41% of children aged 9-13 surveyed said they feel stressed either most of the time or always because they have too much to do. And more than three-quarters of those surveyed said that they wished they had more free time.[18]

Now, don't misread me. There is a great value in extracurricular activities. Kids learn teamwork, discipline, and social skills. Some studies correlate physical play with improved intelligence.[19] Each of us would be wise to count the benefit of involving our children in a variety of extracurricular activities.

That being said, we would also be wise to consider the costs associated with overscheduling children.

More and more families are eating dinner on the fly, often grabbing fast food on their way to soccer practice or music lessons. Unhealthy eating habits aside, this robs many kids of the important, life-influencing opportunity of simply eating together and discussing the day.

Overscheduled kids miss out on an opportunity for extended free play. Free play allows kids to burn off energy and learn social skills in an unstructured environment. It provides opportunity for kids to exercise their imagination, create games, and refine rules. It forces children to learn awareness, police themselves, and develop empathy.

Overscheduled children lose the space to simply be with themselves and learn the art of being alone. In our noisy, busy world, the importance of developing the life skill of solitude, meditation, and quietly being with oneself can not be overstated.

Children need an opportunity to explore their world and themselves. They should be provided the space to discover their own passions and talents. Overscheduling kids from one activity to another often stunts their development in this area.

Just like Jana's story above, it would be wise for us to rethink the heavy scheduling of our children.

Discover New Habits.

What strategies might we as parents implement to eliminate the schedule clutter that results in this overscheduling for both our kids and our own lives? I will offer eight ideas. Likely, you already do some of the action items presented here. But also, there are likely some new habits to consider as well.

Know where the motivation is coming from: you or your child. Take a step back and honestly evaluate the activities, teams, organizations, and clubs your child is enrolled in. Is the underlying motivation truly the welfare of your child? Or are there personal motivations shaping your decisions: succumbing to pressure, trying to impress other parents, or trying to make up for missed opportunities in your own childhood?

Determine an ideal baseline number of activities. Without consulting your calendar, ask yourself this question: "Ideally, how many hours each week should my child be involved in structured, organized activities outside of school?" This will likely vary by age, personality, and need. Once a baseline has been determined, compare this with your current calendar. Are the numbers close? Or do adjustments need to be made?

Elevate the importance of family dinnertime. According to the American Dietetic Association, eating together as a family during adolescence is associated with lasting positive dietary choices in the future.[20] Eating together as a family promotes relationship, understanding, and love. It provides opportunity for kids to digest not only their food, but also the events of the day. Elevate its importance. Guard it. Most likely, you will not be able to eat together every night of the week. But using it as a reference point in your decision-making will provide a valuable filter in saying yes or no to future opportunities.

Schedule time for yourself to be with them. The most important influence in their life is you. You love them the most and know them the best. Too often, we take this for granted and just assume we will find quality time with them as we go our separate ways. But quality time does not occur without the presence of quantity time.

Leave space between events. A spaced-out calendar is more enjoyable than one crammed too tight. In your weekly calendar, create space. Sometimes, this may mean waking early or eating early to relieve the anxiety of rushing out the door. Other times (vacations for example), this may display itself by scheduling one less activity each day—or adding "walk to the bakery" instead.

Develop a family, weekly routine. Help your kids navigate their schedules by establishing a weekly schedule. Some scheduled events are difficult to move: school, sports practices, religious activities. Others are more flexible: weekly chores, bathing schedules, play dates. Intentionally establish a family routine that children can learn to rely on each week.

Reduce your personal commitments. Embrace the seasons of life. There are times in our lives when we are more available than others. Raising young children is an important responsibility and will require time. Provide yourself with the necessary space to do it well by removing less-important commitments from your personal schedule. You'll be glad you did. You can never get the time back once it's gone.

Remember the importance of leaving room to add. If our schedules are so full with no room for margin, there is no opportunity to add something new or something better (whether that be joining a gym, getting to know the neighbors, or handling a family crisis). A too-full calendar leaves no room for addition. Although adding things may seem counterproductive to someone reading a book about decluttering, it is in fact, one good reason to remind ourselves of the importance of creating a margin.

Wise parents take their role seriously. They seek desperately to develop talents, skills, and self-sufficiency in their children. However, they realize fully this does not occur best within the confines of a cluttered schedule.

Free Your Home.

Start here: Is your family schedule too busy? If not, is it trending in that direction? Or have you found victory in this area and settled on an appropriate schedule?

How many evenings a week are you together as a family for dinner? Is that enough? Or do you desire more?

Make a list of every extracurricular activity your children are involved in. If you were forced to remove two of them, which activities would you choose? Why would those be the first to go?

As you evaluate your own motivations for including your child in different activities, do any selfish pursuits begin to arise? Or are each of your choices motivated out of what is best for your child?

[16]
Preparing for Baby

Stories of Change: *Nicolle W., Baltimore, MD*

Nicolle fought decluttering her possessions for a long time. In fact, after getting married and moving her household items into her husband's house, she resisted going through the boxes for over two years. Only recently, after discovering she is pregnant for the second time, has she sold the last of the furniture she was holding on to.

Becoming a mom has had a profound impact on her life and her view of clutter. Staying at home with her child has brought new opportunity to organize and sort out a house full of possessions. But she has fallen in love with owning very little. Nowadays, she has very few things of her own left: a book case full of books and a wardrobe of clothes in varying sizes (pre-pregnancy, between-pregnancy and post-pregnancy).

Despite the progress, Nicolle claims becoming entirely clutterfree is not a goal she will achieve anytime soon. In part, due to the presence (and presents) of an overly generous grandparent. And by her own admission, she still continues to struggle with clothing and linens. But she has come to see in new ways how little is actually needed.

She buys very little now because she recognizes they don't need it. And looks forward to the continuing challenge of remaining clutterfree as the boys get older.

Change Your Thinking.

One of my favorite writers exploring the intersection of motherhood and simplicity is Rachel Jonat. Rachel is the author of *The Minimalist Mom's Guide to Baby's First Year* and the founder of *The Minimalist Mom (.com)*. I asked if she might be willing to write some helpful words for expecting mothers who desire to remain clutterfree.

She offers a very well-rounded approach. I'm confident you will find it encouraging and helpful in rethinking your preparations for a new baby:

Sleep deprived new parents are an easy target for marketers. I know. I was recently a new parent myself. In the early months I bought into the idea that a musical sea horse could soothe my son better than I could. They were empty promises and, before finding simple living, my home was filled to the brim with baby items (most of them unused).

What I've learned since then is that the best thing you can do for yourself, and your new baby, is to slow down. The best way to prepare for a new baby is not with an afternoon of shopping or obsessing over paint samples for the nursery. The best way to prepare for a new baby is to build a community, unburden your schedule, and most of all, relax.

Discover New Habits.

Rachel offers seven ways to prepare for a new baby. No shopping required.

Slow down. Soon enough your days and nights will be turned upside down. The weeks and months leading up to the arrival of a new baby shouldn't be filled with long to-do lists. This is not a time to start a major renovation, move houses, or overburden your schedule. It's a time for long walks, sleeping in, and spending time with loved ones.

Build a community, not a registry list. Your neighbor with four grown children or your new friend from a childbirth class will be more help to you when your baby arrives than any battery operated baby soothing device. Fill your life with friendships and forget about filling closets and rooms with baby paraphernalia.

Relax. Let go of the need for perfection. The nursery details, the accent pillows, and wall murals won't be noticed as you rock your baby to sleep in the dark. The little life that is joining your family won't care if her socks don't match her outfit, but she will care that your arms are steady and your voice is soothing.

Spend more time selecting your healthcare providers than shopping for a stroller. This goes for your Obstetrician, Midwife, Pediatrician, and anyone else involved in your care. Rather than asking your friends what's in their diaper bag, ask them about their experience as a patient. Ask about their child's doctor, their time at a hospital or birthing center, and if they'd recommend their Obstetrician or Midwife.

Sleep. Yes, you'll get a lot of advice from other parents to sleep now because you're about to lose anything close to a normal sleep pattern. And while it's great advice, you should think of prioritizing sleep as not just about 'stocking up' but about creating a new habit. If you're expecting a new baby you should get into the habit of catching sleep when you can. Work on your napping skills and make sleep a priority.

Borrow, don't buy. The first year of a child's life is filled with rapid growth and changes. What amused and delighted your three month old may be of no use just a few weeks later. Whenever possible, borrow any needed items from family and friends. Most people are only too happy to find a home for their unused bassinets, play mats, and booster seats.

Give. A strong element of building a community and a supportive circle of friends and family, is giving. Give your time, give your attention, and give whatever goods and financial contributions you can. Lend your ear to a friend in need, bring a meal to a family when their new baby arrives, and give what you can. Give without expectation. Give because it feels good. Give because you can. And when your growing child outgrows clothes, toys, or supplies, keep your home clutterfree by passing them on to someone else.

Free Your Home.

Is this a chapter that currently applies to your stage in life? If so, great. If not, do you know of any expecting mothers who would benefit from it? Please, by all means, pass this book along to them.

If you are currently expecting (or hope to be soon), what practical steps other than shopping do you consider important enough to make a priority in your life?

Do you have helpful relationships in place with friends, family, or neighbors?

Section 3
Free Your Life

[16]
Keeping Clutterfree Momentum

"Wanting less is a better blessing than having more."
—*Mary Ellen Edmunds*

People sometimes ask, "How do you keep from wanting the stuff that everyone else has?" To be honest, I rarely struggle with that desire anymore. But when I do, I try to remember one thing:

Since deciding to live with less, I have less clutter in my home, less stress in my life, more time for my family, more generosity in my spending, more energy for my passions, more contentment in my heart, more gratitude in my soul, and far more opportunity to pursue things of greater worth.

Immediately, the consumer-based desire begins to fade. When it does, a new question begins to emerge: *Why would I want what everyone else has when they all want what I already possess?*

Overcoming Consumerism.

Owning less brings great benefit to our lives. But wanting less brings even more.

Removing ourselves from the culture of consumption that surrounds us allows wonderful habits to emerge in our lives: contentment, gratitude, freedom from comparison, and the opportunity to pursue greater significance.

Breaking free from excessive consumerism is an essential step not just for a simplified life, but for any life that desires to be lived intentionally. How then can we realize this freedom and what steps can we take to break free?

I have come to realize this is not an easy step for people and there are no easy shortcuts. Consumerism has been branded into our hearts and souls our entire lives. It is going to take more than a few pages in a book to overcome it. But I believe strongly that given the chance to understand and embrace these following principles, it can be overcome in our lives.

Believe it is possible. There are numerous people throughout history and the present who have adopted a minimalist lifestyle. They have rejected materialism and overcome consumerism. Find motivation in their example and know you can join their ranks. Victory always begins there.

Adopt a traveler's mentality. When we travel, we take only what we need for the journey. As a result, we feel lighter, freer, more flexible. Adopting a traveler's mindset for life provides the same benefit—not just for a weeklong vacation, but in everything we do. Adopt a mindset that seeks to carry only what you need for the journey.

Become acutely aware of the consumer-driven society in

which we live. Our world will lead you to believe your greatest contribution to society is the money that you spend. We are faced with 5,000 advertisements every day calling us to buy more.[21] As a result, average consumer debt equals $8,000/household, shopping malls outnumber high schools, Americans spend more on jewelry and shoes than higher education, and 93% of teenage girls rank shopping as their favorite pastime.[22] Recognizing the consumeristic mindset of our world will not immediately remove you from it, but it is an absolutely essential step in the journey.

Compare down. As we begin comparing our lives and possessions to those around us who have more, we lose joy, contentment, and happiness. And we begin trying hard to close the gap. This is because we always compare upward — looking at those who have more. But we could begin breaking through the consumerism-trap if we would begin taking greater notice of those who own less yet remain joyful in their circumstances.

Consider the full cost of your purchases. Usually when we purchase an item, we only look at the sticker price. But this is rarely the full cost. Our purchases always cost us additional time, energy, and focus (cleaning, organizing, maintaining, fixing, replacing, or removing). Making a habit of intentionally factoring those expenses into our purchases will allow our minds to make more competent and confident decisions about our consumption habits.

Realize your money is only as valuable as what you choose to spend it on. The financial resources we have earned or been given hold great potential. They can be used to provide for those without. They can be used to bring justice and hope to a world desperately searching for both. And we ought to dream bigger dreams for our money than the clearance rack at a department store.

Turn off the television. Television glamorizes all that it needs to glamorize in order to stay in existence. Corporations don't spend $50 billion every year on television advertisements because they *think* they can get you to buy their product; they spend that money because they *know* they can get you to buy their product.[23] Television is an industry built on the assumption that you can be convinced to spend (and overspend) your money. You are not immune. We'll discuss this aspect in greater detail in the next section.

Make gratitude a discipline. Gratitude serves little purpose as merely a response to positive circumstances. Gratitude holds its greatest potential as an attitude in undesired circumstances. Embrace it as a discipline during seasons of plenty and seasons of want. Begin focusing more on your blessings than your troubles.

Practice generosity. The surest path to contentment is generosity. Giving forces us to recognize all we possess and all we have to offer. It allows us to find fulfillment and purpose in helping others. Remember, generosity always leads to contentment with far greater efficiency than contentment leads to generosity.

Renew your commitment daily. We are bombarded every single day with more and more advertisements. Rejecting and overcoming consumerism is a daily battle. Expect it to be such. And recommit every morning—or every hour if necessary.

To exist is to consume. But we were designed to accomplish things far greater. And the sooner we remove ourselves from overconsumption, the sooner we realize our truest potential. May it be so in your life and in mine.

Breaking the Influence of Advertisers.

The task of living a simple, clutterfree life is complicated enormously by modern propaganda. Commercials and advertisements work tirelessly to convince us products manufactured on assembly lines will bring us joy and make us insanely happy. But in reality they make us more insane than happy.

The goal of Madison Avenue is to prompt discontent, increase desire, and change our attitude from "That's extravagant" to "That would be nice" to "I really want that" and finally to "I've got to have it."

They are so subtle at their craft we hardly realize we are being brainwashed. Subconsciously, they take control of our desires, our checkbooks, and our life. To stop letting advertisers control our lives, we must be mentally prepared to counter their assault.

One recurring theme throughout this book is the truth that possessions do not equal joy (and you thought you were just buying a book about organizing clutter).

We need to remind ourselves over and over again happiness is not an item to be purchased, it is a decision to be enjoyed. Our happiness is not based on our possessions. Some of the most joyful people I have ever met live in poverty, while some of the wealthiest people I know are miserable. In fact, many times our possessions actually keep us from truly living and enjoying our life. Decide today to be happy.

We ought to vigilantly identify what advertisements are really trying to sell us. The emphasis in modern advertising has moved from providing 'factual' information on a product to creating associations in the mind of a consumer. Most advertisements are not trying to sell us on the material properties of the item; instead, they try to appeal to our subconscious desires (status, sex, prestige, happiness, appearance, self-esteem, identity, or reputation) or subconscious fears (loneliness, security, weaknesses, uncertainty). Be aware of their strategy, look for it, and don't be fooled by it.

We should emphasize buying things for their usefulness, not their status. Purchase items for their ability to meet your needs not for their ability to impress your neighbor. Apply this principle everywhere, but your house, your car, your clothes, and spending on your children are good places to start.

Intentionally and purposefully, we should remove advertisements from our lives as much as possible. Cancel your junk-mail (both physical and digital). Mute your radio/

TV during advertisements or better yet, stop watching television altogether. Enjoy outdoor recreation (biking, exercising, hiking, gardening, camping) or occupy your mind with reading, art, conversation, philosophy, or meditation.

Make it a habit to enforce a 30-day wait period on major purchases. The extra month will provide ample opportunity to answer the question, "Do I really need this?" It will also help you answer these questions: "Are there any subconscious motives to this purchase?," "Which brand is the highest quality?," "Can I find it cheaper elsewhere?," and "How likely is it this purchase will soon become unused?"

And please, join the joyful revolution. It seems that more and more people these days are choosing to say "no" to the mindless collection of material possessions and are saying "yes" to living simple lives instead. Overwhelmingly, these people are adamant that life is better on the other side of consumerism. Join us. And know you are among friends.

[16]
Clutterfree Parenting with Intention

"Parenting is a thinking man's game." —*Mike James*

Parenting requires energy, strategy, and intentionality. Yet, many parents are unwilling to give it the attention it deserves. As a result, their children become shaped by the world around them rather than by the parents who love them.

If you have children, consider what you want your child to become. What values should be most important? What character traits would you most like to see in them? What life skills are most essential? What type of worldview should they have? How should they treat others? Is there a work ethic you would like to instill? Which disciplines are the most important to develop?

Then, go about making it a reality in their lives.

Envision the type of person you would desire them to become. Model that behavior for them. Your words will ring completely hollow without your actions backing them up.

Praise and correct. Observe your children. Notice when their actions and attitudes are consistent with your desires and praise accordingly (over and over again). When their actions or attitudes stand in conflict with the ideals you are hoping to instill, correct gently. Remain consistent.

Provide opportunities for them to grow. Seek out opportunities for your children to learn the lessons you ، desire to teach them. Desire spiritual children? Find a religious institution. Hoping for children who love nature? Spend time outdoors. Want a child who cares for justice? Volunteer at a local homeless shelter. Think this through carefully and be intentional about finding these places for them to grow.

Do your best and let them choose. Parenting is 100% parents trying to shape lives and 100% children choosing their own life. Strategic parents give time, energy, and intentionality to raising their children but give them the freedom to make their own decisions. It is a difficult balance that varies from child to child with no set rules (unfortunately).

Finding Pride and Joy in the Journey.

A few years ago, my daughter walked into our living room carrying the book, *Green Eggs and Ham* by Dr. Seuss. I can still picture its distinct orange cover held against her body by her 5-year old arms. She climbed into my lap, asked if she could read to me, and began opening the front cover. With little hesitation, I agreed. It's important to me that Alexa enjoys reading. And I looked forward to helping her through it.

Little did I know my help would not be needed. Using the sight words she had learned from her kindergarten teacher and simple steps to get through the tricky words (look at the picture, sound out the first letters, look for rhyming words), my daughter successfully navigated every single word in the book. Spoiler Alert: He ends up liking the green eggs and ham at the end.

When my daughter closed the back cover to the book, she looked at me with a huge sense of accomplishment. And when she did, she looked directly into the eyes of the only person smiling bigger than her. I can remember looking down with a feeling of pride I could never communicate with words. The compliments were genuine and the hug was sweet. My daughter was learning to read. She knew it. I knew it. And there was great joy to be found at this point in her knowledge.

Now, just to be clear, I know full-well her journey to become a reader is not complete. *Green Eggs and Ham* is hardly the highest piece of literature she will learn to read… after all, *Pinkalicious* is right around the corner. Being able to sound out every word in a Dr. Seuss book is hardly the culmination of her education. I will still encourage her and challenge her to reach new heights and seek higher accomplishments.

But in this moment, at this time, overwhelming joy and pride were perfectly accurate responses. My daughter had grown much in her ability to read over the previous weeks and months. She had worked hard to reach this point. Her progress deserved to be celebrated. And, she understood there was joy to be found in this journey.

Too often, we live our lives from destination to destination. We look back and mark the significant accomplishments as the milestones that define our lives: a graduation, a new job, a move, or overcoming a tragedy. We look back with fondness and we look desperately forward to the completion of the next: the accomplishment of a life goal, a significant desired award, a major life transition, finding the love of our life, or emerging from one of life's dark valleys triumphant.

Unfortunately, life is not lived exclusively in these destinations. In fact, it is far more often lived in the pathways between them. Consider the fact that these destination moments are few, but the journeys between them are long. These moments between destinations are where we prepare ourselves—and are prepared—to accomplish the goal, to weather the storm, and to choose the next destination carefully.

But because we live in a results-oriented world, finding pride and joy during these moments between destinations is difficult, but absolutely essential.

Notice opportunities for pride and communicate it whenever possible. When your daughter goes through her room before the holidays and picks out a toy to give to those less fortunate, celebrate her decision. When your son notices something out of place in the house and puts it away, praise him for it. Always praise the little steps.

Very likely, your child's life (and probably yours too) deserves far more celebration than you offer. Our lives are not measured by the leaps and bounds as much as they are measured by the little steps and decisions we make every day.

Keep striving forward to become a better person, a better parent, a better citizen, and a better contributor to the world around you. Strive for the great accomplishments that you and the world will use to define your life. But don't be so quick to discount the progress you have already made. Because that's where life is lived. And that's where joy is to be found—in your life and your child's.

Embracing Countercultural Lives.

We live in a culture that begs us to conform. Through its various messages, it calls us to squeeze into its mold. It exerts external pressure on our minds to believe in and buy its opinions, hopes, and aspirations. Yet, the pursuits that define most of our culture never fully satisfy our heart and soul.

In response, the world will tell us to just run faster, reach further, work harder, make more, and become conformed more deeply. But its promised offer of fulfillment always remains out of reach. Our deepest longings are left unsatisfied.

Unfortunately, through this vicious cycle, we lose our uniqueness. We lose our passion. We lose our energy. We lose our opportunity to choose a different future. And because we are too busy chasing the wrong things, we sacrifice our opportunity to find something greater and more fulfilling in this life.

Meanwhile, our heart begs us to live differently. Our spirit calls us to seek our own passions. But all too often, the external pressure from the world calls us back into conformity. And we reenter the race. How do we break free?

More importantly, how do we help our kids break free?

We help them understand there must be more. We come to a point where we realize there is more to life than what the world is peddling. We admit we have foolishly bought what the world is selling—and our lives are still empty. Possessions have not brought happiness. Money has not provided security. Popularity and power have not satisfied. And sex has not brought love. The answers clearly do not lie in a life conformed to the unoriginal culture of our day. We know it to be true. And we seek desperately for teachable moments to transfer this understanding to our kids.

We limit culture's messages into their lives. Calls for conformity enter through our eyes and ears, take room in our mind, and force out the pleas surfacing from within our soul. While we can never remove the external pressure completely, we can limit their opportunity for impact. We can watch less television. We can flip through fewer ads. We can worship fewer celebrities. And as we begin to reduce the noise from the outside in their lives, we open space in their mind to hear from the inside.

We support them in pursuing newfound passions. To break free from conformity, we must realign our lives to seek our heart's truest desires. If our lives do not intentionally chart a course in this new direction, they will eventually revert back to their original state. Take heart, no one knows every step of the journey ahead. We only need to know the first one.

We can teach them to listen more to their heart. In the absence of external noise, we find opportunity to intentionally search our heart. We find the space to allow our soul to speak and cry out for its desires. We hear best in solitude, meditation, and self-examination. Be advised, this is difficult at the beginning. We are rarely flattered with what we find at first. Model solitude and meditation for your children. Learn it yourself. And pass it on to them.

Nobody knows for certain where our hearts will lead us. Our souls must speak for themselves. And giving up control is one of the most difficult aspects of parenting.

Teach your kids to reject blind conformity. Because when they do, rarely will they discover their heart desires more money, possessions, fame, or power. It will usually ask for something far more countercultural than those.

Helping Kids Overcome Envy.

One common stumbling block for parents in the journey to clutterfree is the notion that they need to protect their children from envy. They fear because their home will not be filled with all the latest and greatest products on the market, their children will become jealous of other kids.

But our role as parents is not to eliminate the opportunity for envy. Our role is to parent our kids intentionally and train them to think mindfully about envy and learn to overcome it.

This past summer, I drove my son and five of his neighborhood friends to a restaurant to celebrate his birthday. Each of the boys live in close proximity to one another, but they still represented a wide range of socio-economic classes. As might be assumed, the conversations in the vehicle covered a wide range of topics, but one conversation emerging from the back seat piqued my interest a bit more than the others.

Two boys in the back seat began comparing their lives with one another. I knew, of course, this was not a rare conversation—I had similar conversations while I was growing up. But what I found particularly interesting (and prompted my eavesdropping) was the level of mutual envy surfacing.

At first, the comparison was on video gaming systems and who owned more games. Then, a discussion on what type of cars their parents drove surfaced, followed by a conversation on house size. Eventually, the comparison turned to athletics and sports teams and girls. Each time, one participant hoped to one-up the other.

I learned an important parenting lesson that day: You cannot outpace envy. The game of comparison and envy and jealousy is a game that can never be won. Among those who choose to play, there are no winners—only losers. No one can have it all and no one can ever buy enough things to eliminate envy. There will always be something to be jealous about.

Instead, we must teach our kids how to handle envy and how to overcome it. It is important we help them learn how to focus on the positive, the shortsightedness of comparison, and the foolishness of jealousy. We should teach them to be generous and grateful, and to celebrate the success of others.

Envy will always hold our children hostage. As parents, we need to equip them to break free and experience a more fulfilling life because of it.

Raising Consumer Conscious Teenagers.

Five years ago, we sold, donated, or discarded most of our material possessions. It was a decision based on discontent with our current lives. We realized we had far too few resources left over for the things most important to us.

Since embarking on this life-giving journey, we have found the lifestyle resonates effectively with young adults, parents, and older generations. But one of our greatest passions has also been to inspire teenagers to build a better life by owning less.

For the last 15 years of my life, I have given my life to teenagers through my full-time employment in nonprofit organizations. I have developed relationships with hundreds of teens. I have spoken at public schools and student conferences. I have written books for teenagers. In short, I love the opportunity to invest in their lives and introduce them to a better way to live.

There are, of course, significant challenges in reaching teenagers with the message of simplicity. The world around them grows increasingly materialistic. Teenagers value acceptance and conformity with their peers. Advertisers target their message to the young adult demographic. Teenagers are beginning to explore their own decision-making. As a result, they are less likely to value input from others—particularly parents.

The challenges are certainly formidable.

But we find great motivation by also recognizing the benefits of reaching teenagers with this message.

Many of their most significant decisions are still ahead of them. The message of simplicity helps equip them to make wise ones.

They are not in debt—yet. As a result, they are not held captive under the weight of creditors (especially housing, cars, student loans).

Their spending habits are not yet formed. They are definitely being shaped, but are not fully determined.

We must recognize the challenges before us. But we also understand the importance of sparing our teenagers from decades of financial burden and empty promises of fulfillment. We recognize an important opportunity to inspire teenagers to pursue lives of greater value.

I have spoken with parents, mentors, and community members around the country about this opportunity. I have taken countless pages of notes. When I began comparing these notes, I noticed several key themes developing. For everyone's benefit, I have included them below.

Together, they form a blueprint for parents, mentors, and community members to steer children away from consumerism and toward simplicity instead.

Model simplicity. The cliche rings true, "Life lessons are better caught than taught." The first (and most important) step in raising minimalist teenagers is to model for them the joys and benefits of intentionally living with less.

Encourage idealism. Many teenagers embrace idealism and desire to find a cause that can change the world. But far too often, teenage idealism is misunderstood and/or discouraged. It ought to be encouraged. Allow children of all ages to dream bigger dreams than cozy homes, cool cars, and white picket fences.

Volunteer as a family. Be active offering your time in the community through a local food bank, soup kitchen or community organization that serves the underprivileged in your area.

Watch less television. It's not as hard as you think—and has immediate results.

Make teenagers pay for expensive items themselves. Every parent ought to provide food, clothing, shelter, and basic necessities. And every parent should give good gifts to their kids. But asking your teenager to purchase expensive items with their own money will create a stronger sense of ownership and a better understanding of the relationship between work, money, and consumerism.

Encourage teenagers to recognize the underlying message in advertising. Advertisements are not going away and can never be completely avoided. Help your child read behind the marketing message by often asking, "What are they really trying to sell you with this advertisement? Do you think that product will deliver on its promise?" If luck is in your favor, it can even become a fun little game in your family.

Find an ally. By the time your children have reached the teenage years, your role as a parent has changed significantly. In most families, teenagers are beginning to express independence in their relationship with their parents —but that doesn't mean they won't listen to anybody. Find an accompanying voice in your community that aligns with your values and provide opportunities for him/her to speak into your teenager's life.

Discourage entitlement in your family. Often times, as parents, we work hard to ensure a significant advantage for our children by providing for them at all costs. But as we do, we equally run the risk of not preparing them for life by neglecting to teach them the truths of responsibility. It is hard work maintaining the possessions of life (lawns have to be mowed, cars cleaned and maintained, laundry sorted, rooms tidied). Expose teenagers to this truth as early (and as often) as possible.

Travel to less developed countries. This world is big and the cultures are varied. Some of the most teachable moments of my teenage years occurred while visiting third-world countries and experiencing the living conditions of those who live on so little (an estimated 6 billion people live on less than $13,000/year)[24]. Their joy and peace has served as an inspiration to me even up to this day.

Teach them what matters most is not what they own, but who they are. A man or woman of noble character holds a far greater asset than those who have traded it for material possessions. Believe this truth. Live this truth. And remind the teenagers in your life of it as often as possible.

Our world has chased happiness, joy and fulfillment in the pursuit of riches and possessions for far too long. It is time we intentionally seek to raise a generation that values much greater things.

[16]
Clutterfree with a Reluctant Partner

"Where there is love there is life." —*Mahatma Gandhi*

People who choose minimalist living as a lifestyle may face any number of doubters—these may be friends, colleagues, or parents. But what do you do when the biggest doubter of all is usually your biggest supporter? When the person you have chosen to live life with doesn't see the benefits of your decision? When the person you love the most doesn't support the new you? And the fact that you live together only complicates the issue, you share one space and so does your stuff.

When my wife and I decided to become minimalist, we agreed together to pursue this new lifestyle. But, we've still had plenty of disagreements along the way about how much stuff to unload, how much stuff to keep, and how our purchasing habits would change.

Because we are not always on the same page, we have learned to compromise and figure it out together.

But what should be done when your partner is on the complete opposite side of the spectrum? What about a situation where you are pursuing life with less but your partner is a self-described packrat? How can these two lifestyles coexist?

If this describes your living situation, my heart goes out to you. It is not easy. Couples have split over less, but I hope you won't. Certainly, it is going to take grace, patience, love, and commitment. But then again, commitment always requires those attributes.

Refuse to let stuff separate you. I have heard from a number of people who have taken steps to minimize their belongings, but in the process have become so frustrated with their partner they have allowed strife and resentment to set in. Refuse to let that happen. Remember, you chose clutterfree for a reason—most likely, you desire simplicity because you were frustrated with material things cluttering your life and preventing you from truly living it. You decided you valued other things more than your possessions —like relationships with the people you love. If that is the case, it would be foolish to allow physical things to again come between you and your most treasured relationship. Your loved ones are too important. Realize you can't change someone else. You can only change yourself (and your attitude).

Begin by purging your personal items. Resist the temptation to remove your partner's belongings without permission. Start with your own stuff and minimize as much as you can without treading on shared territory. You may be surprised how much clutter you can remove from your home just by removing your own things.

Let your example speak for itself. Certainly, explain to your partner why you have chosen a lifestyle of owning less. But as much as you desire to debate and verbally convince your partner to choose it too, your actions will always speak louder than your words. Allow the benefits of your clutterfree life to do their own convincing. A clean, clutterfree side of your closet will always be far more convincing than a thorough explanation of the 80/20 principle.[25] And a refreshingly stress-free desktop or nightstand will begin to look very attractive to your partner the first time they misplace something important.

Find common ground. Likely, there are some commonly used areas in your home that you can both agree need some decluttering. Whether it be a junk drawer, a linen closet, the kitchen counters, or the garage, even the worst of hoarders can typically come to the rational conclusion that something can be better organized (no matter how small the area). Ask your partner about specific areas in your home that you would like to declutter. You just may be surprised how verbally supportive they can be when you get specific about what you would like to accomplish.

Be patient. Remember, one of the greatest markings of love is patience. And it's worthwhile to be reminded again...and again..and again.

If their refusal to discard possessions is systemic of deeper issues, tread wisely. It is very possible there may be some deep heart wounds that are causing your partner to be a packrat. Your partner may be insecure about themselves and find their security in the things that they own. Your partner may have such a strong desire to impress others they depend on their belongings for their purpose. Or their hoarding may be a symptom of OCD or another medical disorder. In any case, the correct step is to tread lightly and find your partner the support and help they need.

[20]
Becoming a One-Income Family

First off, I fully realize this is a very personal chapter. For a variety of well-thought-out reasons, not everyone who picks up this book desires to become a one-income family. That's fine. This is not written to change your thinking or convince you otherwise.

Instead, I have included this chapter to encourage those who do desire such a lifestyle. I have known a number of dual-income families over the years who desire to become one-income—typically experienced in conjunction with the birth of a child. This chapter is included at the end to encourage them.

My wife and I have lived our entire married lives (15 years) on one modest income. We have proven it is possible. And if we can accomplish it, so can you.

Eleven years ago, our first child was born. As my wife had always intended, she immediately resigned from her position as an administrative assistant and became a full-time homemaker. At the time, my gross income was less than $40,000/year + health insurance benefits. I offer the numbers only as a frame of reference—there are surely one-income families that live on more and some that live on less. Over the years, I have experienced a number of pay increases (as one might expect), but my career in non-profits was never chosen for its high level of compensation.

Still, we were able to survive and thrive on one-income because we took some very intentional steps with our lives, finances, and decisions. Study this road map below. Decipher your place on it. And then, take the very step you've been desiring all along.

Ask when and why, not if. I'm all for careful planning and crunching the numbers, but I'm also all for taking risks and learning to figure things out. When my wife quit her job to stay at home, we looked at the financial inflow and outflow. But our intentions in analyzing the numbers were never motivated by the question "Is this going to work?" We had already made the decision. The when/why had already been determined. Budgeting was approached as the means needed to make the necessary adjustments to accomplish it —not the determining factor.

If possible, prepare ahead of time. My wife and I received valuable advice when we got married. A good friend of ours said, "Decide now to live off one income, even if both of you are working. Put the entire second income directly into savings." This decision to live off my income alone contributed significantly to our first home's down-payment. But more importantly, it kept our lifestyle at a level that provided options when our first child was born (or if an unexpected job loss would have occurred). If possible, begin making choices today (avoid debt, lifestyle creep, and high mortgage payments) that will accommodate one income in the future.

Be content with less. A one-income family will, by definition, earn less money than a two-income family. The pursuit of possessions will need to be tempered. You'll own a smaller home with less-fancy cars. Luckily, you won't be missing much. There's far more joy to be found in pursuing less than can be found in owning more.

Be convinced of the benefits. There are countless benefits to staying at home with young children that motivated our decision: stability, relationship, experience, educational opportunity, scheduling flexibility, consistent discipline, fewer expenses. We recognized these benefits and used the opportunity to make one-income a reality.

Budget. A healthy understanding of budgeting is required in most every case. But from my experience, there are only a small variety of expenses that keep families from living on one income: too costly mortgage, car payments, eating out frequently, exorbitant entertainment expenses (tickets, vacations, and/or alcohol), and credit card debt. Start there and you'll solve 90% of your financial problems. To embrace healthy budgeting techniques, you'll find countless budgeting tools online. The one that works best is the one that actually provides you with the tools to live within it. Additionally, a one-income family is one that treats all incoming revenue as "shared," not "yours" or "mine." If you need to change your thinking on this, do it now.

Find an outlet for relationship. One difficulty of removing oneself from the workforce is the loss of a built-in network of relationships. Interpersonal relationships with peers are absolutely essential to our well-being. Be intentional in seeking out a place to find them: church, community groups, mom/dad groups, activity groups, etc.

Find an outlet for service. You have gifts, talents, experiences, and education that our world needs. Likely, you still desire to use them. Just because you have decided to stay at home does not mean you resigned from using your gifts to change the world. Look for opportunities to use them on a broader scale. There are, after all, countless organizations (schools, community, nonprofits) that need your giftedness. Find one as an outlet for your talents.

Embrace temporary or part-time. If there are some internal reasons keeping you from fully becoming a full-time, stay-at-home parent, consider the options of part-time or temporary. You don't need to leave the workforce permanently. You can still keep a toe in it by finding a part-time employment arrangement that fits your schedule/ desire. And as your family becomes more self-reliant, you can always make the decision to return back to work.

Again, a one-income living arrangement may not be the perfect solution for every family, but it has worked well for ours on a relatively modest budget. And because it has worked for us, I know it is completely achievable for you.

[21]
Stop Comparing Your Life.
Start Living It.

"Comparison is the thief of joy." —*Theodore Roosevelt*

I've struggled with it most of my life. Typically, I blame it on having a twin brother who is five inches taller with much broader shoulders. But if I was being truly honest, more likely, it is simply a character flaw hidden somewhere deep in my heart.

I've lived most of my life comparing myself to others. At first, it was school and sports. But as I got older, I began comparing other metrics: job title, income level, house size, and worldly successes.

I have discovered there is an infinite number of categories upon which we can compare ourselves and an almost infinite number of people to compare ourselves to. Once we begin down that road, we never find an end.

Comparison often stands as one of the most difficult hurdles in seeking to live a life with fewer possessions. In a world desperately focused on proving worth through the acquisition of material possessions, choosing to live with less can be difficult. If we get too caught up in comparing ourselves to others, we will never have victory in living clutterfree.

This tendency to compare ourselves to others is as human as any other emotion. Certainly I'm not alone in my experience, but it is a decision that only steals joy from our lives. And it is a habit with numerous shortcomings.

Comparisons are always unfair. We typically compare the worst we know of ourselves to the best we presume about others.

Comparisons, by definition, require metrics. Only a fool believes every good thing can be counted (or measured).

Comparisons rob us of precious time. We each get 86,400 seconds each day.[26] And using even one to compare yourself or your accomplishments to another is one second too many.

You are too unique to compare fairly. Your gifts and talents, successes, contributions, and value are entirely unique to you and your purpose in this world. They can never be properly compared to anyone else.

You have nothing to gain, but much to lose. For example: your pride, your dignity, your drive, and your passion.

There is no end to the possible number of comparisons. The habit can never be overcome by attaining success. There will also be something—or someone—else to focus on.

Comparison puts focus on the wrong person. You can control one life—yours. But when we constantly compare ourselves to others, we waste precious energy focusing on other peoples' lives rather than our own.

Comparisons often result in resentment. Resentment towards others and towards ourselves.

Comparisons deprive us of joy. They add no value, meaning, or fulfillment to our lives. They only distract from it.

Indeed, the negative effects of comparisons are wide and far-reaching. Likely, you have experienced (or are experiencing) many of them first-hand in your life as well. How then, might we break free from this habit of comparison?

Consider, embrace, and proceed forward with the following steps:

Take note of the foolish (and harmful) nature of comparison. Take a good look at the list above. Take notice of comparison's harmful effects in your life. Find priority to intentionally remove it from the inside-out.

Become intimately aware of your own successes. Whether you are a writer, musician, doctor, landscaper, mother, or student, you have a unique perspective backed by unique experiences and unique gifts. You have the capacity to love, serve, and contribute. You have everything you need to accomplish good in your little section of the world. With that opportunity squarely in front of you, become intimately aware of your past successes. Find motivation in them to pursue more.

Pursue the greater things in life. Some of the greatest treasures in this world are hidden from sight: love, humility, empathy, selflessness, generosity. Among these higher pursuits, there is no measurement. Desire them above everything else and remove yourself entirely from society's definition of success.

Compete less. Appreciate more. There may be times when competition is appropriate, but life is not one of them. We have all been thrown together at this exact moment on this planet. And the sooner we stop competing against others to "win," the faster we can start working together to figure it out. The first and most important step in overcoming the habit of competition is to routinely appreciate and compliment the contribution of others.

Gratitude, gratitude, gratitude. Gratitude always forces us to recognize the good things we already have in our world.

Remind yourself nobody is perfect. While focusing on the negatives is rarely as helpful as focusing on the positives, there is important space to be found remembering that nobody is perfect and nobody is living a painless life. Triumph requires an obstacle to be overcome. Everybody is suffering through their own obstacles, whether you are close enough to know it or not.

Take a walk. Next time you find yourself comparing yourself to others, get up and change your surroundings. Go for a walk—even if only to the other side of the room. Allow the change in your surroundings to prompt change in your thinking.

Find inspiration without comparison. Comparing our lives with others is foolish. But finding inspiration and learning from others is entirely wise. Work hard to learn the difference. Humbly ask questions of the people you admire or read biographies as inspiration. But if comparison is a consistent tendency in your life, notice which attitudes prompt positive change and which result in negative influence.

If you need to compare, compare with yourself. We ought to strive to be the best possible versions of ourselves—not only for our own selves, but for the benefit and contribution we can offer to others. Work hard to take care of yourself physically, emotionally, and spiritually. Commit to growing a little bit each day. Learn to celebrate the little advancements you are making without comparing them to others.

With so many negative effects inherent in comparison, it is a shame we ever take part in it. But the struggle is real for most of us. Fortunately, it does not need to be.

On the other hand, the freedom found living clutterfree is life-giving and unmistakable. Discover it today.

Endnotes

1 *The Survey of Consumer Payment Choice* (Boston, MA: Federal Reserve Bank of Boston, January 2010), 53.

2 Calculated by dividing the total revolving debt in the U.S. ($801 billion as of December 2011 data, as listed in the Federal Reserve's February 2012 report on consumer credit) by the estimated number of households carrying credit card debt (50.2 million).

3 Robert Weagley, "One Big Difference Between Chinese and American Households: Debt," Forbes (June 24, 2010); accessible at forbes.com/sites/moneybuilder/2010/06/24/one-big-difference-between-chinese-and-american-households-debt. Retrieved December 11, 2013.

4 Paul Lukas, "Our Malls. Ourselves," Fortune Magazine via CNN Money (October 18, 2004); accessible at money.cnn.com/magazines/fortune/fortune_archive/2004/10/18/8188067/index.htm. Retrieved December 11, 2013.

5 Jon Mooallem, "The Self-Storage Self," The New York Times (September 2, 2009); accessible at nytimes.com/2009/09/06/magazine/06self-storage-t.html. Retrieved December 11, 2013.

6 Naomi Seldin Ramirez, "America's Clutter Problem Fueled Self-Storage Industry," Albany Times Union (September 8, 2009); accessible at http://blog.timesunion.com/simplerliving/americas-clutter-problem-seen-in-storage-units/14455/. Retrieved December 11, 2013.

7 Daniel Ray, "Credit card statistics, industry facts, debt statistics," Credit Cards (November 14, 2013); accessible at http://www.creditcards.com/credit-card-news/credit-card-industry-facts-personal-debt-statistics-1276.php. Retrieved December 11, 2013.

8 Angela Johnson, "76% of Americans are living paycheck-to-paycheck," CNN Money (June 24, 2013); accessible at http://money.cnn.com/2013/06/24/pf/emergency-savings. Retrieved December 11, 2013.

[9] Elizabeth Fletcher, "Too many toys can have a negative effect on children," The Signal: Georgia State University NewsPaper (February 24, 2010); accessible at http://www.gsusignal.com/opinions/too-many-toys-can-have-a-negative-effect-on-children-1.2167665#.Uqxuv6Up-ap. Retrieved December 13, 2013.

[10] Anna Weinstein, "Why Good Friendships Matter," Education.com (September 17, 2008); accessible at http://www.education.com/magazine/article/Good_Friendships/. Retrieved on December 11, 2013.

[11] Courtney Carver, Project 333; accessible at http://theproject333.com/about/. Retrieved December 11, 2013.

[12] Mattias Wallander, "Closet Cast-Offs Clogging Landfills," Huffington Post (April 27, 2010); accessible at http://www.huffingtonpost.com/mattias-wallander/closet-cast-offs-clogging_b_554400.html. Retrieved on December 11, 2013.

[13] U.S. Department of Labor, "Consumer Expenditures--2012," Bureau of Labor Statistics (September 10, 2013); accessible at http://www.bls.gov/news.release/cesan.nr0.htm. Retrieved at December 13, 2013.

[14] Steven Dowshen, MD, "Teaching Good TV Habits," Kids Health (October, 2011); accessible at http://kidshealth.org/parent/positive/family/tv_affects_child.html#. Retrieved on December 13, 2013.

[15] Mayo Health Clinic, "Children and TV: Limiting your child's screen time," Mayo Clinic (Aug. 16, 2013); accessible at http://www.mayoclinic.com/health/children-and-tv/MY00522/NSECTIONGROUP=2. Retrieved on December 13, 2013.

[16] Kaiser Foundation, "Daily Media Use Among Children and Teens Up Dramatically From Five Years Ago," Henry J Kaiser Family Foundation (January 20, 2010); accessible at http://kff.org/disparities-policy/press-release/daily-media-use-among-children-and-teens-up-dramatically-from-five-years-ago/. Retrieved on December 13, 2013.

[17] Firestone, Robert, The Self Under Siege: A Therapeutic Model for Differentiation. Taylor and Francis. New York City, NY, 2013. pg. 151.

[18] Unknown, "Are today's kids too busy?," Hudson Valley Parent; accessible at http://www.hvparent.com/articlepost.aspx? id=386&c=3&t=ARTICLE. Retrieved on December 17, 2013.

[19] Dan Peterson, "Exercise Improves Kids' Academics," Live Science (December 29, 2008); accessible at http://www.livescience.com/5249-exercise-improves-kids-academics.html. Retrieved on December 17, 2013.

[20] Jennifer Starky, "Eating Together as a Family Creates Better Eating Habits Later in Life," Journal of the American Dietetic Association (September 2007); accessible at http://www.eurekalert.org/pub_releases/2007-09/ada-hft082907.php. Retrieved on January 4, 2014.

[21] Louise Story, "Anywhere the Eye Can See, It's Likely to See an Ad," New York Times (January 15, 2007); accessible at http://www.nytimes.com/2007/01/15/business/media/15everywhere.html?pagewanted=all&_r=0. Retrieved on December 17, 2013.

[22] *Affluenza.* Prod. CWK Network. PBS. 2006.

[23] Unknown, "Ad Spending," Local Media Marketing Solutions (Q2 2013); accessible at http://www.tvb.org/trends/4705. Retrieved on December 17, 2013.

[24] Jane Vessels, "The World of Seven Billion: How and Where We Live.," National Geographic (March, 2011); Interactive map accessible at http://ngm.nationalgeographic.com/2011/03/age-of-man/map-interactive. Retrieved on December 17, 2013.

[25] The Pareto principle (also known as the 80–20 rule) states that, for many events, 80% of the effects come from 20% of the causes.

[26] Your watch.

becoming
((• minimalist.com

Looking for continued inspiration? Becoming Minimalist is dedicated to rational minimalism and discovering what that uniquely means for each person.

The website welcomes hundreds of thousands of regular readers each month—and there are thousands of new readers every day discovering the site for the first time.

If this book is your first introduction to our message, welcome. I hope you found the book to be encouraging, inspiring, and helpful. Please pass it along to someone else.

Becoming Minimalist is designed to inspire you to pursue your greatest passions in life by owning fewer possessions. It is based on the realization that there are far more important things to accomplish in life than buying and owning possessions.

The more people introduced to this life-changing message, the better. Our world needs to hear it! Because if we only get one life to live, we might as well make it the best one possible.

Find us online:

Website: www.becomingminimalist.com
Facebook: www.facebook.com/becomingminimalist
Twitter: www.twitter.com/joshua_becker
Digital Newsletter: www.becomingminimalist.com/newsletter/

Made in the USA
San Bernardino, CA
05 June 2015